# EUROPEAN COSTUME

## OF THE SIXTEENTH THROUGH EIGHTEENTH CENTURIES

*in Full Color*

150 Illustrations

Edmond Lechevallier-Chevignard

DOVER PUBLICATIONS, INC.
NEW YORK

## Bibliographical Note

This Dover edition, first published in 1995, includes all 150 color illustrations from *Costumes historiques des XVI*$^e$, *XVII*$^e$ *et XVIII*$^e$ *siècles*, published by A. Lévy, Paris, 1867 (see Publisher's Note for further details). The Publisher's Note has been prepared specially for the present edition. The new English captions extract data from the original French text.

### DOVER *Pictorial Archive* SERIES

This book belongs to the Dover Pictorial Archive Series. You may use the designs and illustrations for graphics and crafts applications, free and without special permission, provided that you include no more than four in the same publication or project. (For permission for additional use, please write to Permissions Department, Dover Publications, Inc., 180 Varick Street, New York, N.Y. 10014.)

However, republication or reproduction of any illustration by any other graphic service, whether it be in a book or in any other design resource is strictly prohibited.

## Library of Congress Cataloging-in-Publication Data

Lechevallier-Chevignard, Edmond, 1825–1902.
 [Costumes historiques des XVIe, XVIIe, et XVIIIe siècles. English. Selections]
 European costume of the sixteenth through eighteenth centuries : in full color / Edmond Lechevallier-Chevignard.
  p.  cm.
 "150 illustrations."
 Includes all the illustrations and condensed translations of the text of Costumes historiques des XVIe, XVIIe siècles. Paris : A. Lévy, 1867.
 ISBN 0-486-28519-7
 1. Costume — Europe — History — Pictorial works. I. Title.
GT720.L43  1995
391'.0094 — dc20                                                    95-5988
                                                                        CIP

Manufactured in the United States of America
Dover Publications, Inc., 31 East 2nd Street, Mineola, N.Y. 11501

# PUBLISHER'S NOTE

The present volume reproduces in full color all 150 illustrations from the two quarto volumes published by the Librairie d'Architecture de A. Lévy, Paris, 1867, under the title *Costumes historiques des XVI^e, XVII^e et XVIII^e siècles* (etc.). A full translation of the title follows: "Historic costumes of the 16th, 17th and 18th centuries; drawn by E. Lechevallier-Chevignard; engraved by A. Didier, L. Flameng, F. Laguillermie *et al.*; with a historical and descriptive text by Georges Duplessis of the Imperial Library." The plates were issued in 75 installments before the publication in volumes. Edmond Lechevallier-Chevignard (1825–1902) was a decorative painter and engraver who taught at the Ecole des Arts Décoratifs in Paris.

Slightly more than half the plates are devoted to the sixteenth century; there are about fifty for the seventeenth century, and about twenty for the eighteenth. All were redrawn by Lechevallier-Chevignard from visual sources contemporary with the costumes: drawings, prints, paintings and stained glass. In many cases, the original works were by truly major artists, including such names as Raphael, Titian, Teniers and Goya. Although 150 plates naturally cannot cover the full ground of three centuries, the subjects are extremely varied, covering all walks of life, from kings and popes to peasants, and representing clothing worn by men, women and children in numerous European countries and regions. Civil, military and religious costumes are included.

In the original publication, two pages of French text accompanied each plate. The new English captions in the present edition are condensations of this French text, adding nothing new in the way of interpretation or identification; here and there, first names and life dates of original artists have been newly added. The captions include in each case: the country or region represented; the status or occupation of the person(s) shown; some form of dating (by century; by year; by reign or period; by the lifespan of the original artist); the original visual source (this was lacking in a handful of instances); and the salient features and nomenclature of the apparel illustrated. Names of rulers are regularized in their English form; names of other individuals are given in the appropriate native forms.

Most of the plates appear here two to a page, although hardly any have been reduced from their size in the French publication. For variety, some of the larger and more elaborate images have a page to themselves; most of these have been slightly enlarged. Because of exigencies of page makeup, a few pictures have been slightly moved from their original sequence; the numbering in this volume reflects only the final Dover sequence.

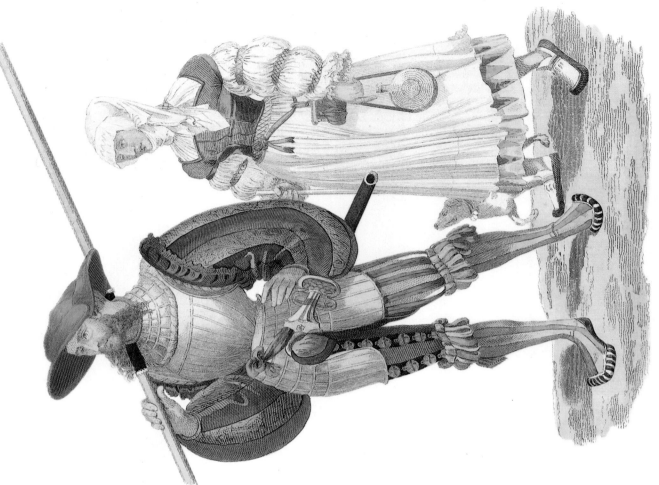

2. German pikeman (landsknecht) and peasant woman, from a hand-colored print by Hans Guldenmund, first half of 16th century. The man wears a steel breastplate, wide sleeves, a broad-brimmed felt hat, multicolored breeches and hose supported by garters. The woman wears two bodices and an overskirt over her dress, a chemisette, separate sleeves and a headcloth fastened with a brooch.

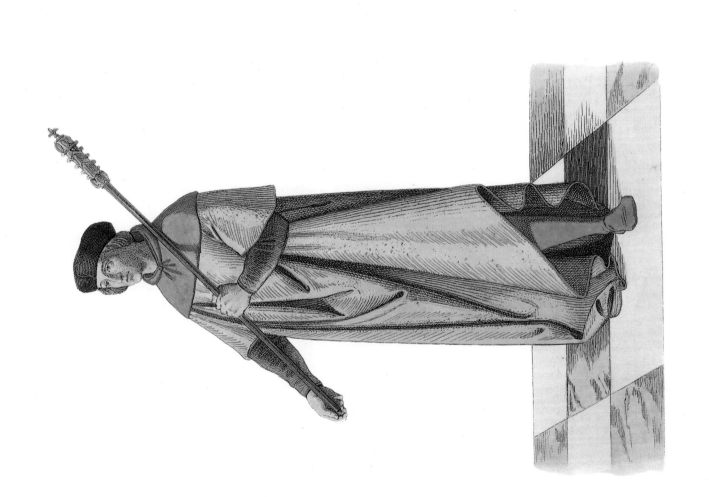

1. Ceremonial mace-bearer, from a French miniature, ca. 1500. Gray cloak and blue collar over a green garment: red hose; black wool cap.

4. German landsknecht playing a fife, from a print by Hans Guldenmund, first half of 16th century. These soldiers dressed fancifully according to their means; compare no. 2.

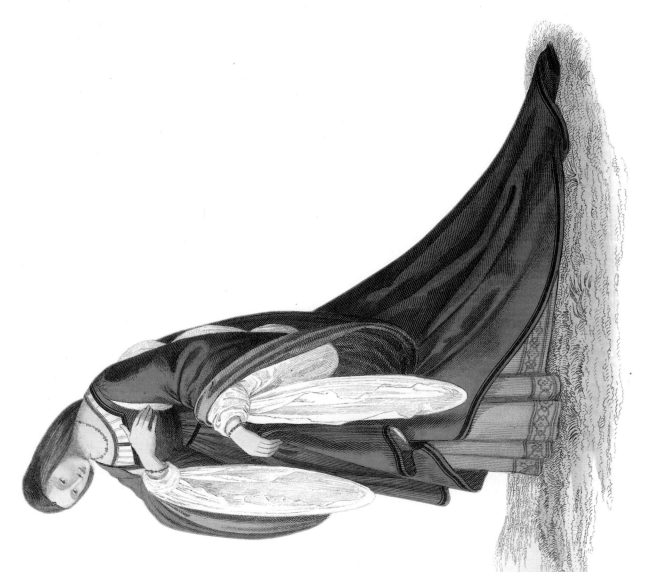

3. Isabella d'Este, Countess of Mantua, from a painting by Lorenzo Costa, early 16th century. Black velvet headband; dress with train gathered in front to reveal the underskirt; puffed muslin sleeve linings.

5. Pierre, Viscount of Rohan, Marshal of France (died 1513), from a contemporary tapestry. His horse's caparison bears the arms of Rohan. The Viscount wears full armor of the period and carries a marshal's baton.

6. Louise of Savoy (died 1532), mother of French king Francis I, from a miniature. Long black dress of flowered damask, black headdress.

7. Pope Julius II (reigned 1503–1513), from a fresco by Raphael. The Pontiff, who is attending Mass, wears a white surplice over a white cassock, with a red mozzetta over his shoulders.

9. Lady-in-waiting at the court of Francis I, from a drawing on parchment. Overdress with train, its fur lining forming mufflike sleeve cuffs.

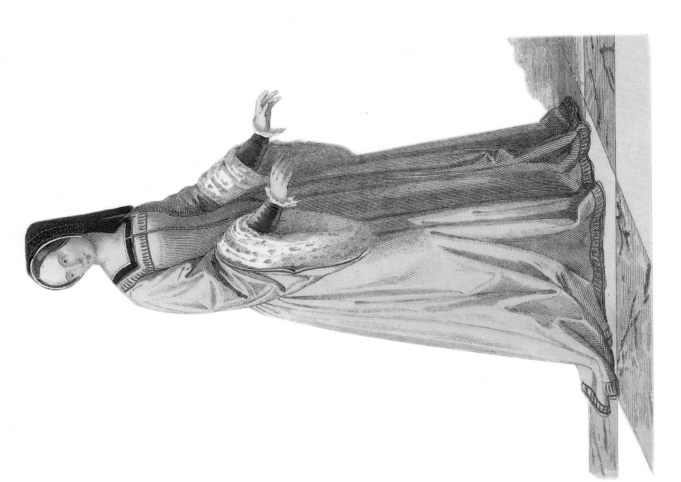

8. Lady-in-waiting at the court of French king Francis I (reigned 1515–1547), from a miniature. Wide, fur-lined sleeves; typically French headdress.

10. Maurice the Brave, Duke and Elector of Saxony (reigned 1541–1553), from an engraving attributed to Lucas Cranach. Red satin robe, with ermine lining and collar.

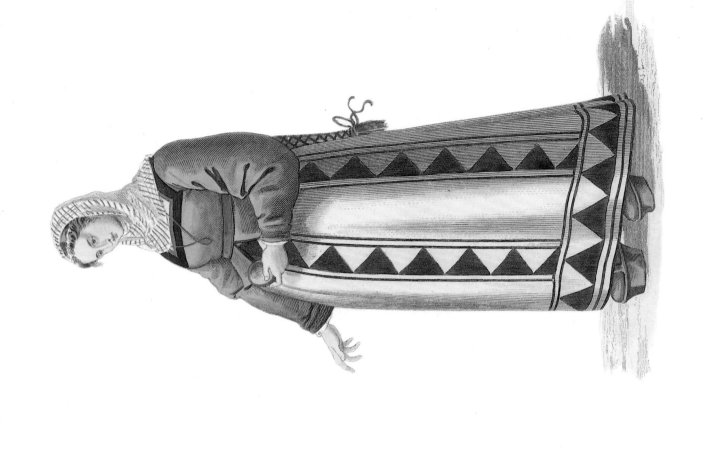

12. Spanish woman from Burgos, from a 16th-century miniature. Wool skirt with triangular appliqués, bodice with tails, braided hair, muslin hood, wooden clogs.

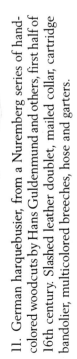

11. German harquebusier, from a Nuremberg series of hand-colored woodcuts by Hans Guldenmund and others, first half of 16th century. Slashed leather doublet, mailed collar, cartridge bandolier, multicolored breeches, hose and garters.

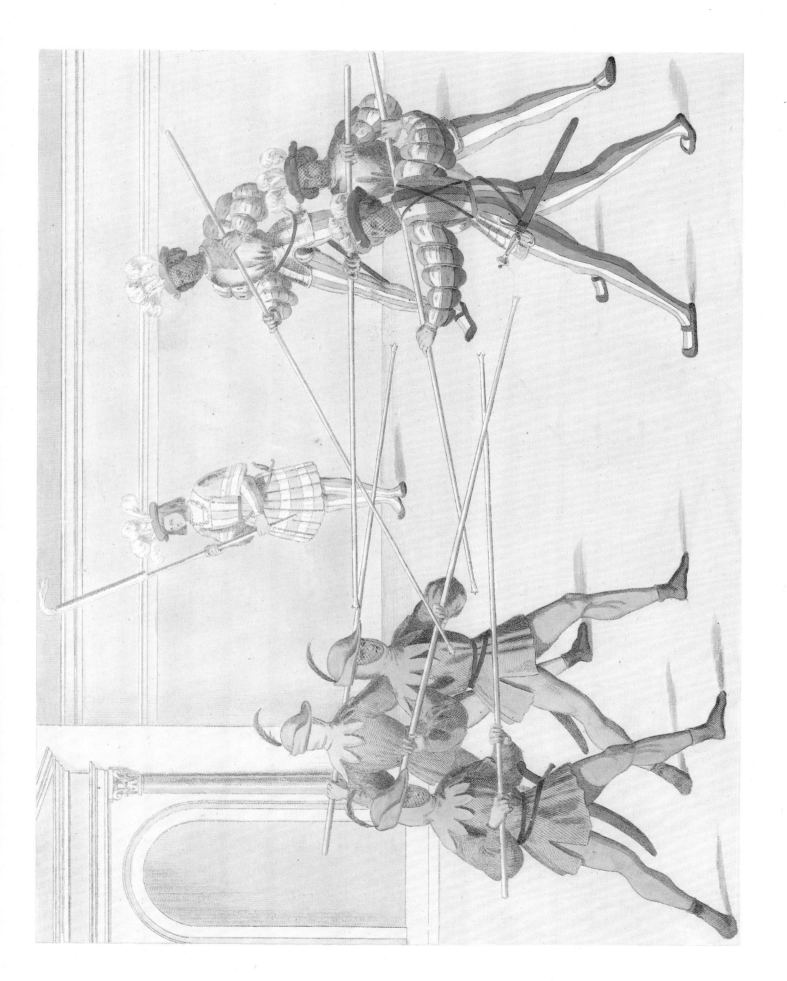

13. Fencing bout at a festival in Nuremberg, ca. 1500, from a series of drawings. Masks and breastplates for protection, team colors and styles for hats, tunics and hose.

15. The artist Hans Sebald Beham, from a self-portrait painted in 1534. Black felt hat; black fur-lined cloak over a red costume.

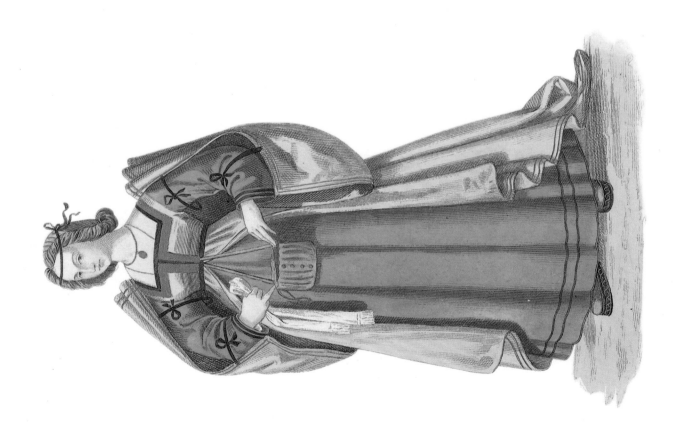

14. Spanish woman from Granada, from a 16th-century miniature. Cape over a dress; hair ribbon and small toque; alms purse.

17. Keeper of hunting hounds during the reign of French king Francis I, from a tapestry. Yellowish tunic over blue smock; blue hose, soft boots and thick-soled overshoes. Royal colors on the dogs' collars.

16. Italian woman from Milan, from a 16th-century miniature. Red skirt divided in three by yellow silk bands; bodice with black velvet bands; slashed sleeves lined with white muslin; silk hair net.

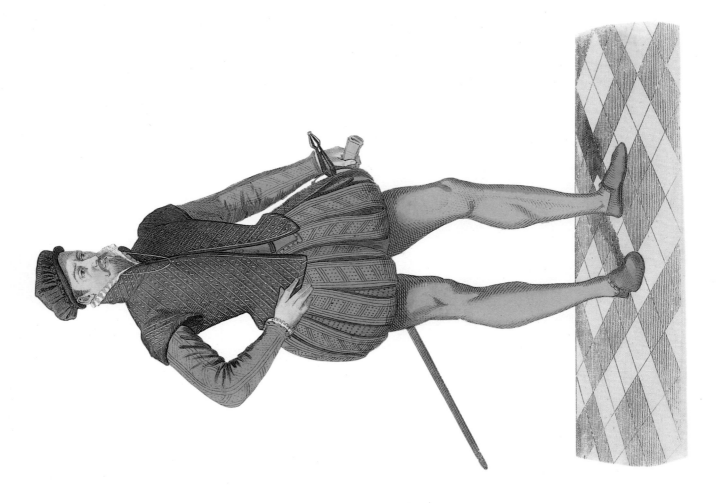

19. Ernest Baumgartner, Nuremberg patrician, 1570, from a painting. He is dressed in the then international Spanish style: form-fitting doublet over a long-sleeved vest, trunk hose, hose, cap.

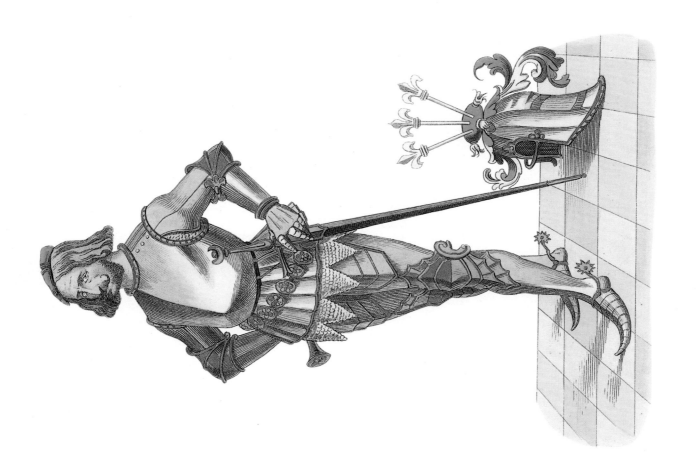

18. Nuremberg patrician of the Strömer family, 16th century, from a book illustration. Full armor: cuirass over coat of mail, brassards, gauntlets, thigh and shin pieces, pointed foot armor with spurs, helmet.

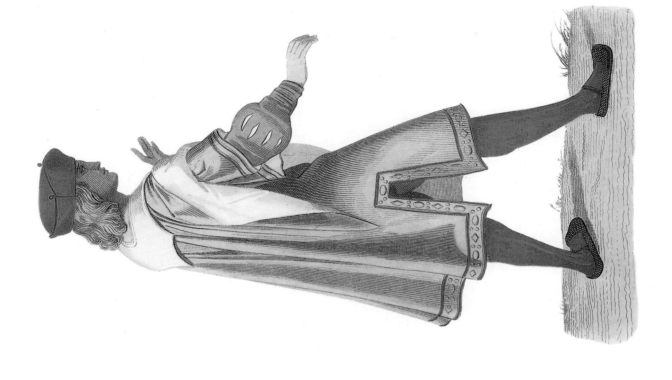

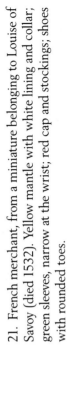

21. French merchant, from a miniature belonging to Louise of Savoy (died 1532). Yellow mantle with white lining and collar; green sleeves, narrow at the wrist; red cap and stockings; shoes with rounded toes.

20. Swiss lady, from a 16th-century miniature. Skirt and over-skirt; two-part sleeves; alms purse; pleated collar; hair in a hood, topped with plumed cap.

22. Halberdier, from a print by Hans Guldenmund, first half of 16th century. Brocade jacket, striped drawers, particolored hose and garters; wide plumed hat over skullcap.

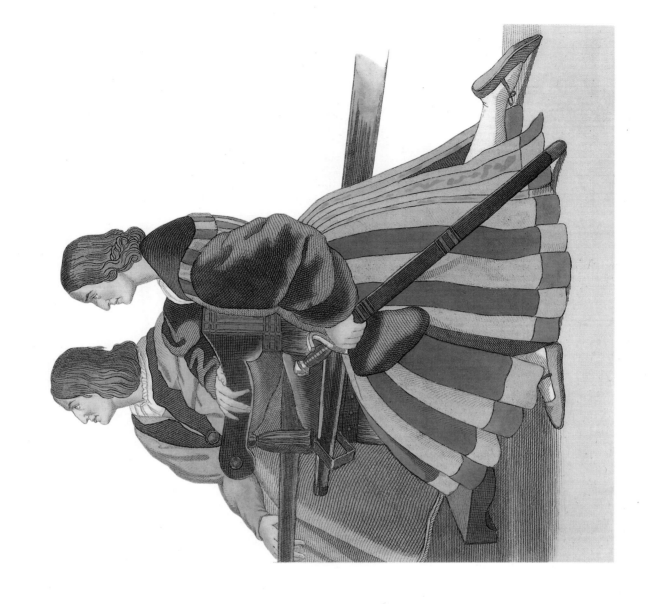

24. Roman gentleman, ca. 1510, from a fresco by Raphael. LEFT: Black silk tunic over orange shirt. RIGHT: Skirt and bodice with attached collar and sleeves; cap.

23. Nuremberg patrician of the Kress family, 16th century. Lacy jerkin over brocade shirtfront; wide sleeves and over-sleeves; skirt, stockings, shoes, plumed hat.

26. Falconer in the service of Francis I, from a tapestry. Jacket, tunic, hose, stockings, hat, game bag, hunting knife, lure for recalling the falcon.

25. Halberdier of the bodyguard of French king Francis I (unit organized 1544), from a miniature. Jacket over multicolored tunic; white hose and shoes; black felt hat with plumes.

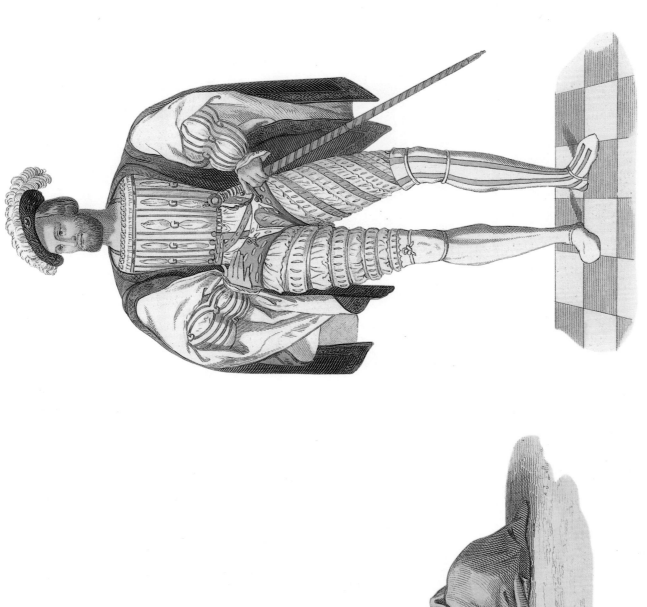

28. Claude de Lorraine, first Duc de Guise (died 1550), from a painting. Court costume: cape over slashed jerkin; hose and stockings of different colors; plumed cap.

27. Citizen of Amiens, from a miniature owned by Louise of Savoy (died 1532). Fur-lined mantle over a jerkin with tight-fitting sleeves.

29. Venetian killing his wife, 16th century, from a fresco by Titian in Padua. Everyday wear of the upper class. The man wears a tunic over a jerkin. The woman wears a chemise and skirt.

30. English nobleman, from a woodcut in Cesare Vecellio's 1590 costume book. Long fur-lined damasked robe, pleated collar, tall felt hat.

31. Noblewoman of Lorraine, from a 16th-century drawing. Long dress with equally long overdress open in front, sleeves puffed at the shoulders, goffered collar, coiffe.

32. German standard-bearer of a private military company, from a 16th-century painting. Doublet, trunk hose, slashed sleeves, ruff, plumed cap.

33. French king Francis I (reigned 1515–1547), from a miniature. Black armor, red velvet skirt. The horse is sumptuously adorned.

34. French joiner, early 16th century, from a miniature. Blue smock over red jerkin; cap.

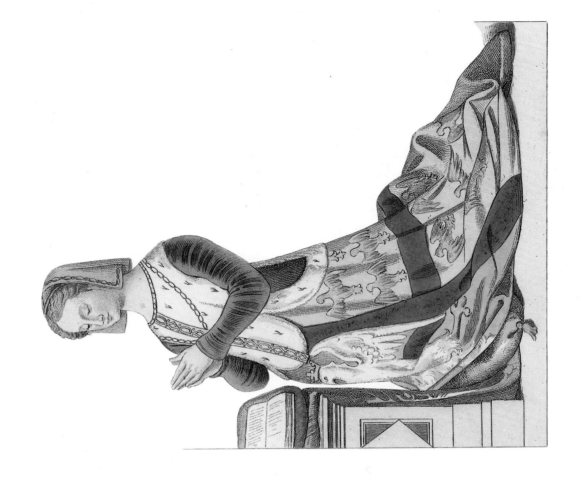

36. Louise de Montmorency, wife of Gaspard de Coligny, from a stained-glass window. Dress with the arms of Montmorency; ermine-trimmed bodice (surcoat); hood.

35. Gaspard de Coligny, Marshal of France (died 1522), from a stained-glass window. Tabard with the arms of Coligny; thigh and shin armor; coat of mail; felt gloves; helmet and gauntlets on the floor.

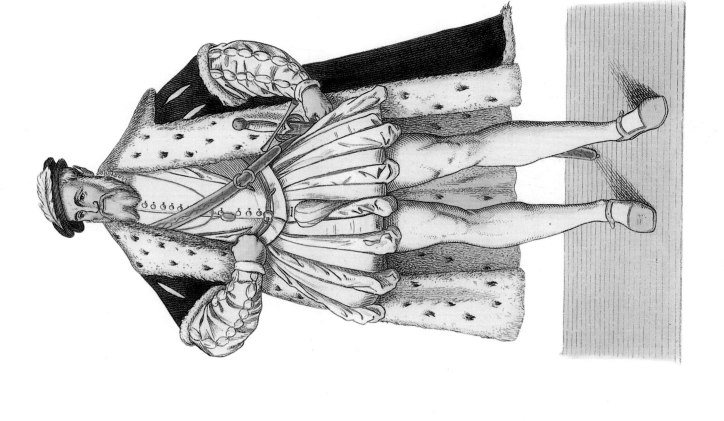

38. François de Lorraine, Duc de Guise (1519–1563), from a painting. Court costume: ermine-trimmed cape, trunk hose, doublet, hose, cap, leather shoulder-belt.

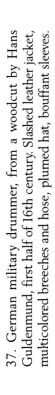

37. German military drummer, from a woodcut by Hans Guldenmund, first half of 16th century. Slashed leather jacket, multicolored breeches and hose, plumed hat, bouffant sleeves.

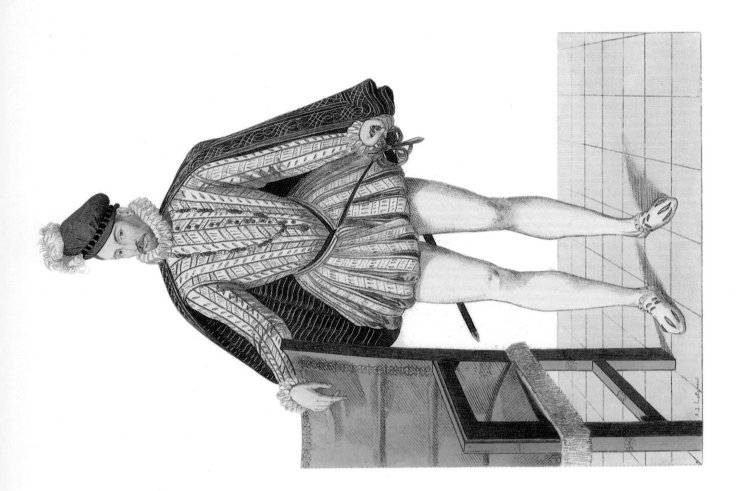

40. King Charles IX of France (reigned 1560–1574), from a painting. Plumed cap, ruff, short cape, doublet, trunk hose.

39. German servant, from a 16th-century woodcut. Hair ribbon, goffered collar, bodice, skirt, apron.

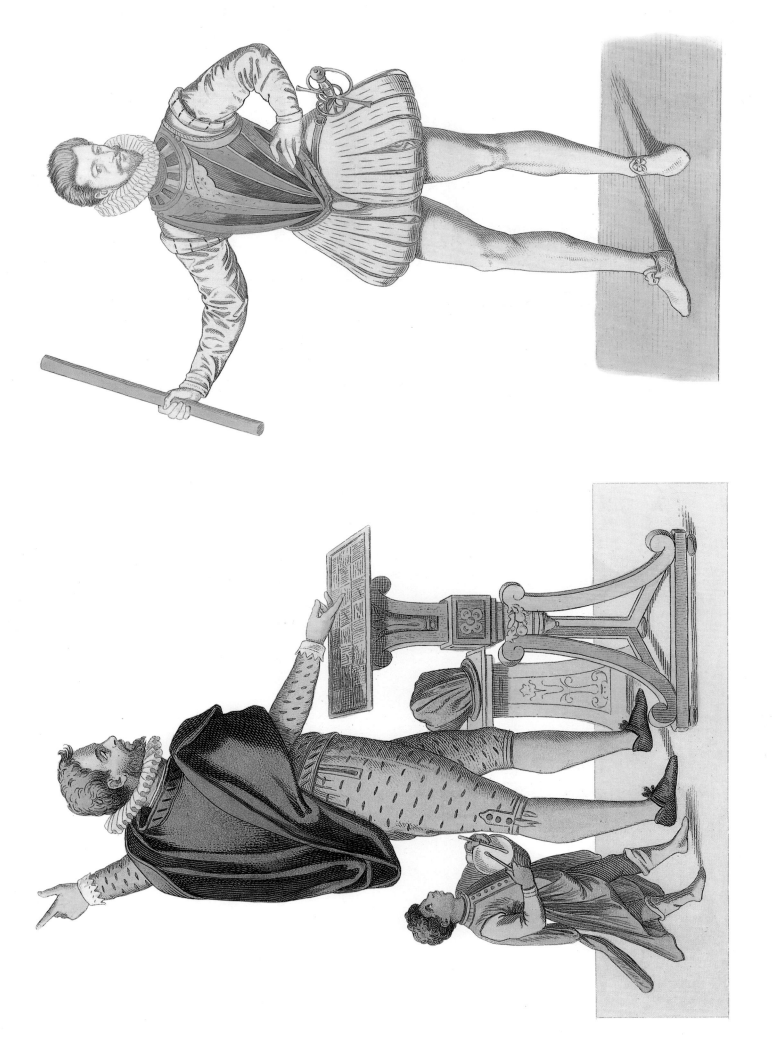

42.  Henri de Lorraine, Duc de Guise, from a painting anterior to 1579. Typical court costume of the period.

41.  Venetian everyday wear, from a book illustration of 1587. Ruff, cape, doublet, breeches, stockings.

47. English man-at-arms, from a 16th-century hand-colored woodcut. Armor over a coat of mail over a leather jerkin; two-handed sword.

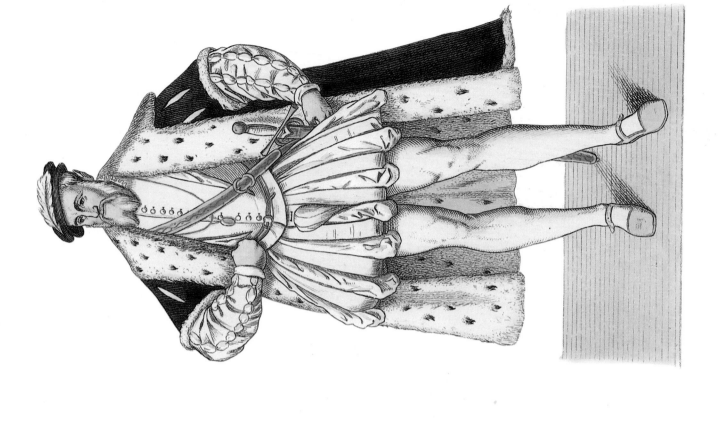

38. François de Lorraine, Duc de Guise (1519–1563), from a painting. Court costume: ermine-trimmed cape, trunk hose, doublet, hose, cap, leather shoulder-belt.

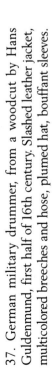

37. German military drummer, from a woodcut by Hans Guldenmund, first half of 16th century. Slashed leather jacket, multicolored breeches and hose, plumed hat, bouffant sleeves.

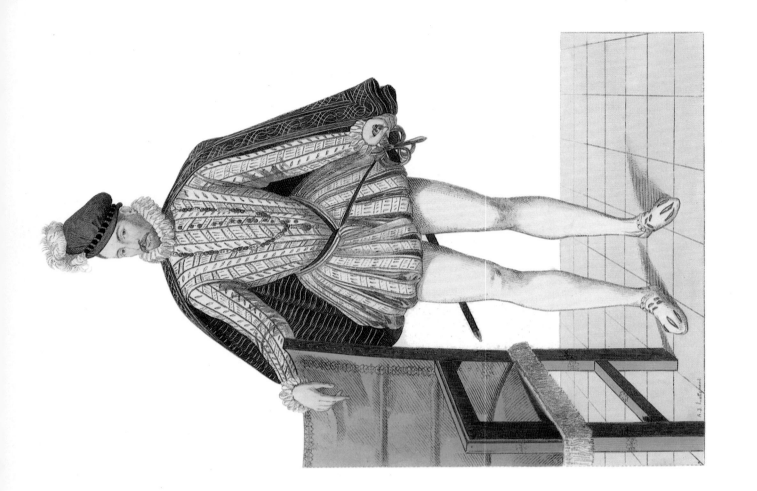

40. King Charles IX of France (reigned 1560–1574), from a painting. Plumed cap, ruff, short cape, doublet, trunk hose.

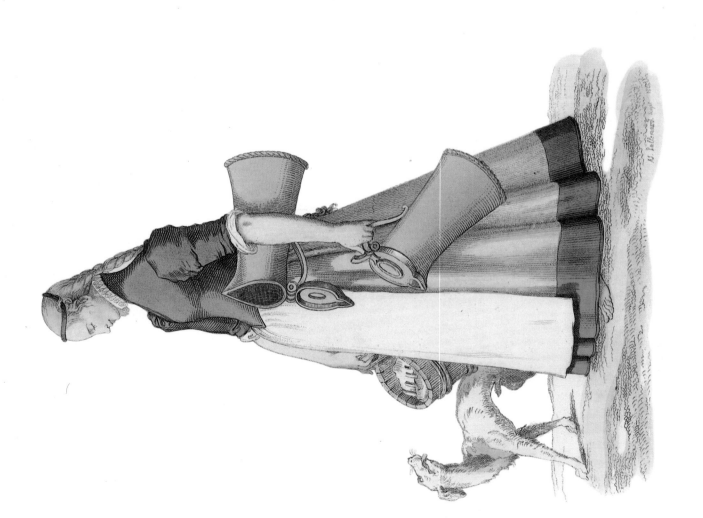

39. German servant, from a 16th-century woodcut. Hair ribbon, goffered collar, bodice, skirt, apron.

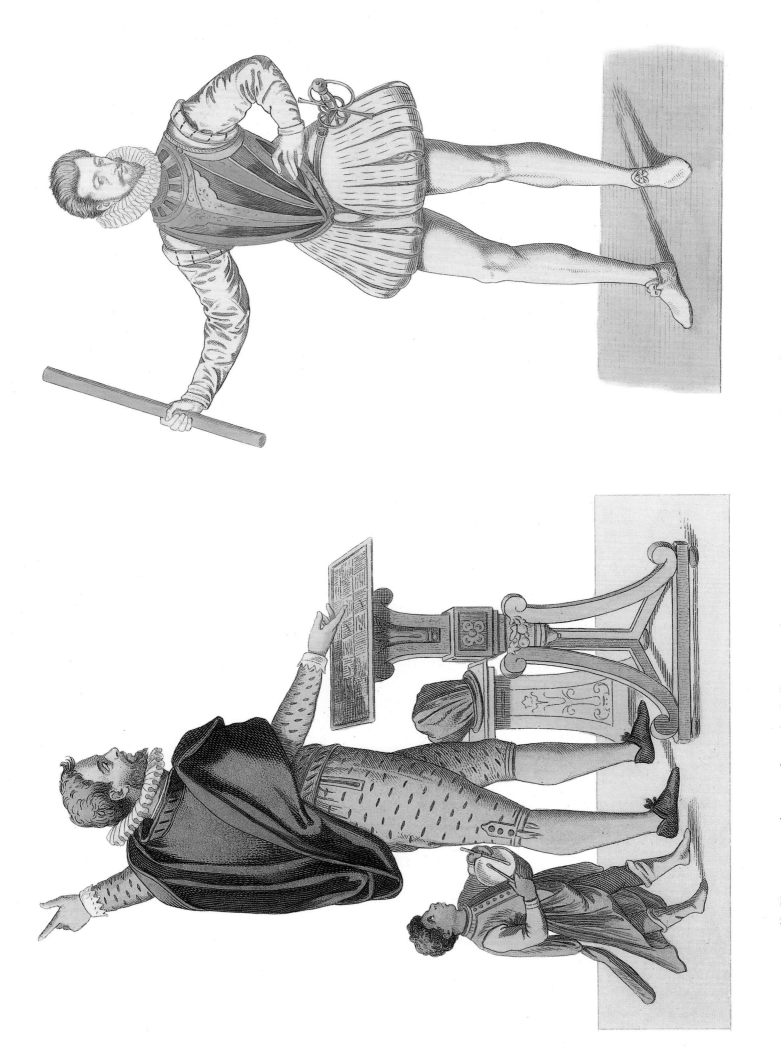

42. Henri de Lorraine, Duc de Guise, from a painting anterior to 1579. Typical court costume of the period.

41. Venetian everyday wear, from a book illustration of 1587. Ruff, cape, doublet, breeches, stockings.

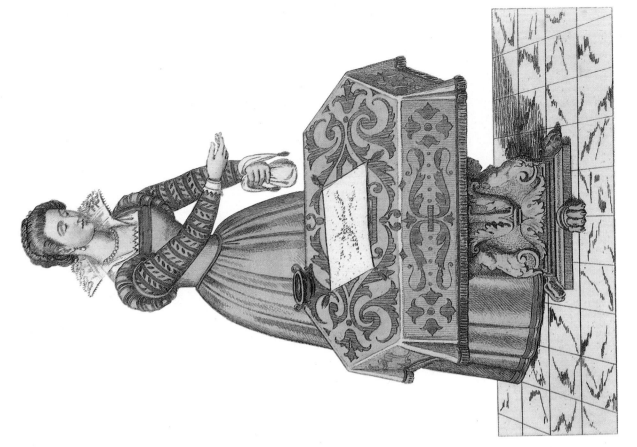

44. Young Venetian woman, from the same book. Fan-shaped collar, close-fitting sleeves, pearl headband.

43. Venetian middle-class women with bags of silkworm eggs, from a book illustration of 1587. Plunging necklines, floor-length dresses.

46. Highborn Italian lady, from a late 16th-century painting. Overdress with slit ornament, lace ruff and cuffs, pearl and sapphire necklaces, pearl headband with aigrette.

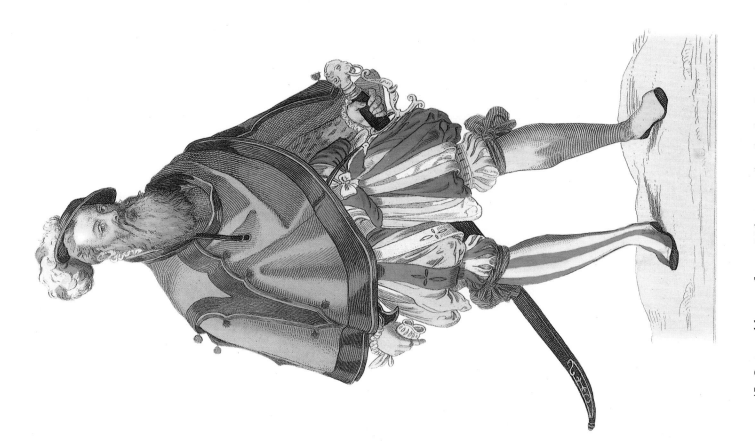

45. Swiss nobleman, from a 16th-century hand-colored wood-cut. Cloak covering a jerkin, breeches and stockings of different colors, plumed hat.

47. English man-at-arms, from a 16th-century hand-colored woodcut. Armor over a coat of mail over a leather jerkin; two-handed sword.

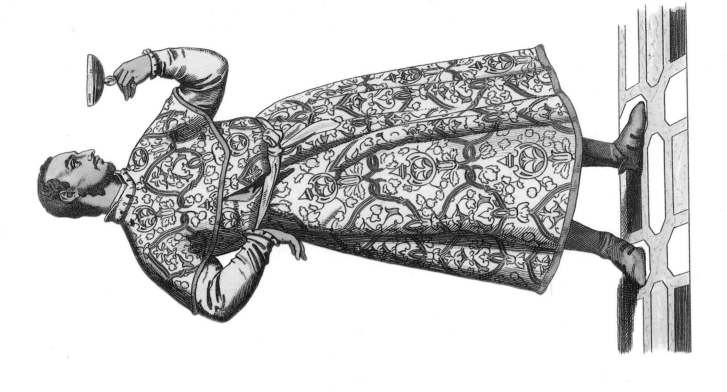

49. Benedetto Caliari, brother of Paolo Veronese, from the latter's painting *The Marriage at Cana*, 1563. Long, embroidered silk-brocade tunic.

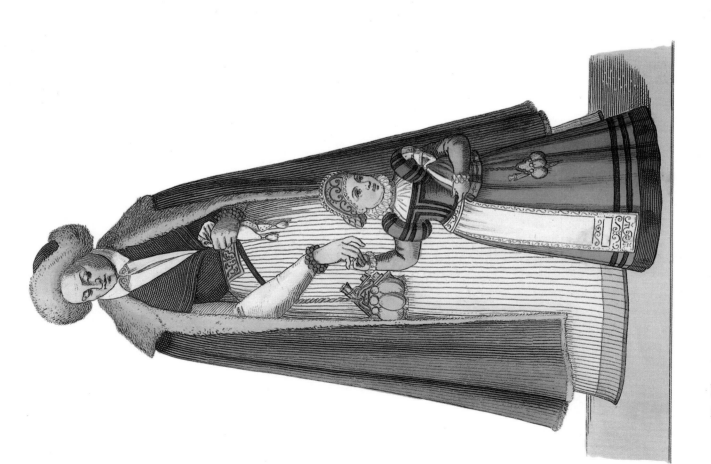

48. Silesian governess and girl, from a 16th-century woodcut. The woman wears a fur-lined cape over a simple bodice and skirt. The girl wears an embroidered apron over a rich bodice-and-skirt outfit.

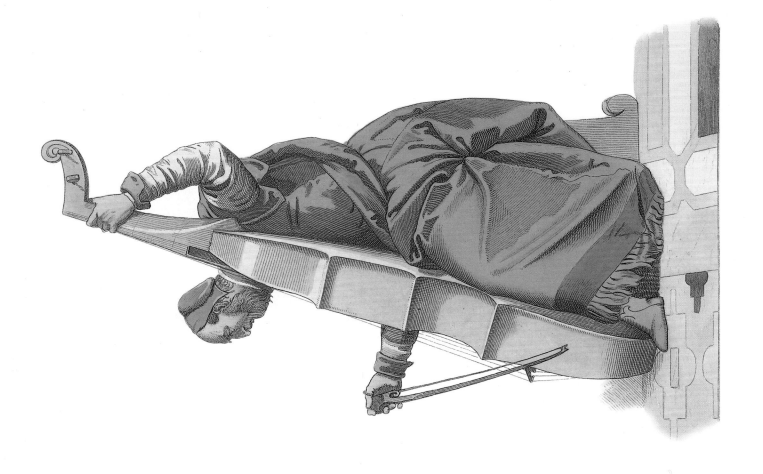

51. The painter Titian as a bass-viol player, from Veronese's *Marriage at Cana*, 1563. Silk cap, voluminous robe.

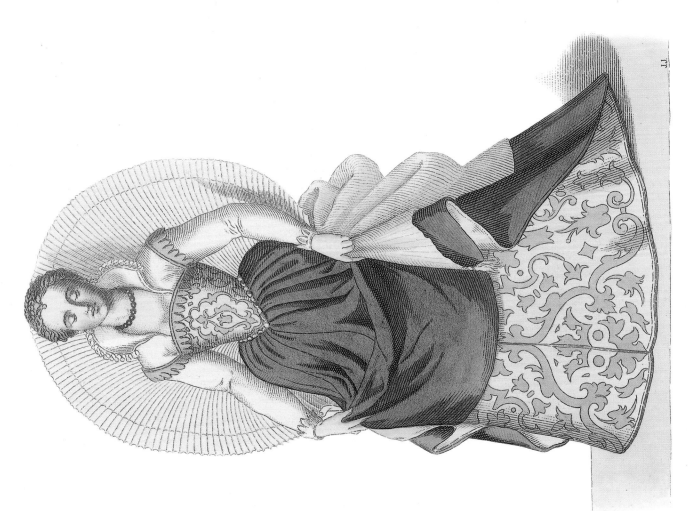

50. Venetian noblewoman, from a 16th-century drawing. Brocade dress with satin overskirt; starched linen veil; pearl waistband.

53. Spanish nobleman, 16th century. Short cape over a jerkin; trunk hose, stockings, goffered collar, tall velvet cap.

52. Italian noblewoman from Ravenna, 16th century. Pearl headband; veil; bodice with sleeves puffed at shoulders and trailing bands; skirt and overskirt.

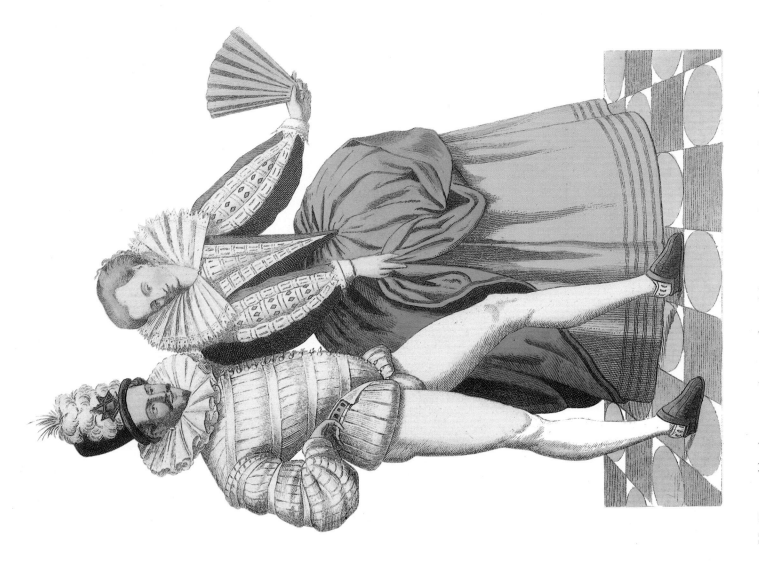

55. Young nobles dancing, at the time of French king Henry III (reigned 1574–1589), from a painting. The man wears doublet, short trunk hose and stockings. The woman wears a dress that is open on the arms and bosom, revealing the chemisette beneath; the underskirt is also clearly visible.

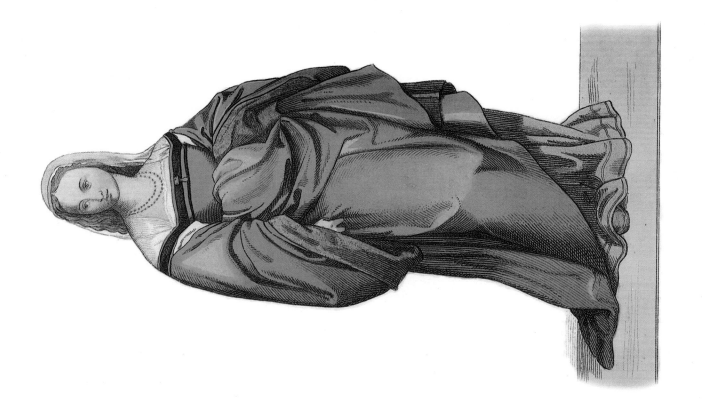

54. Florentine lady, from a fresco by Andrea del Sarto (died ca. 1530). Gathered dress; low-necked bodice revealing the embroidered chemise; veil.

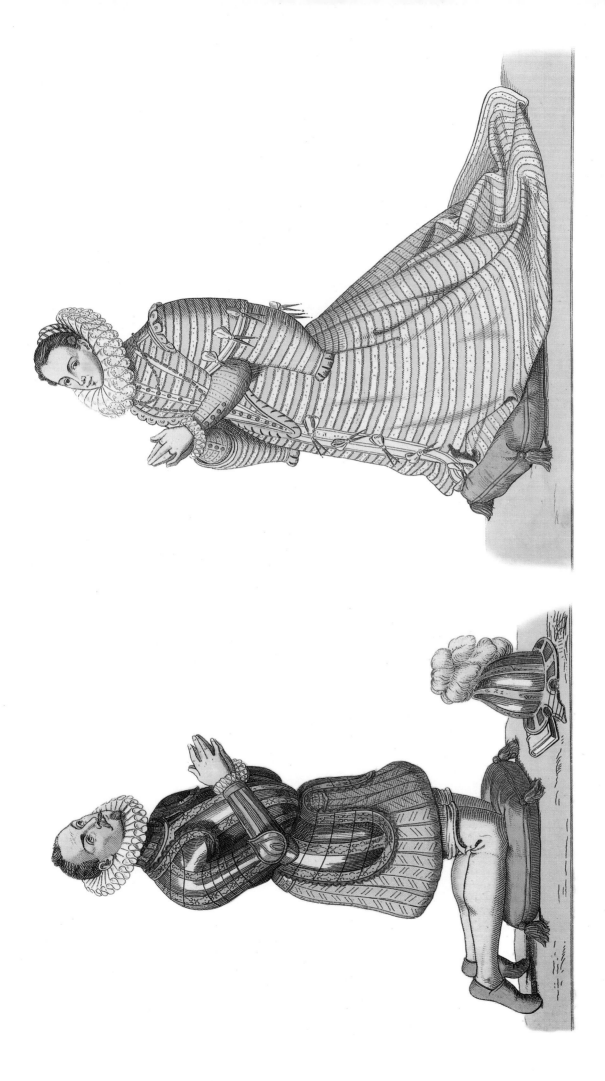

57. Archduchess Isabel Clara Eugenia of Austria, wife of Albert. Long dress; wide sleeves that can either hang loose or be adjusted to the forearm; long bodice, ending in a point; skirt closed with aglets; wide ruff.

56. Archduke Albert of Austria (1559–1621), from a miniature. Gilded steel cuirass, trunk hose, stockings, ruff.

59. Young Englishwomen, 16th century. "Masculine" hat; hair net, goffered collar; long dress of brown wool, only very slightly ornamented, over a muslin chemisette with gold patterning.

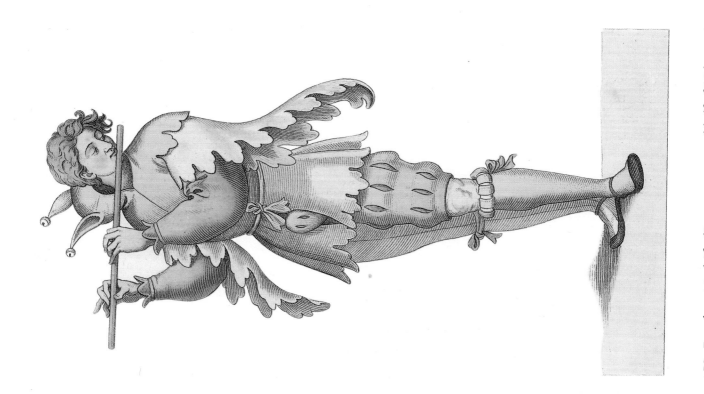

58. French satirical "fool" costume, second half of 16th century, from a woodcut. Tunic with scalloped shoulders and sleeves; the right leg is in a long stocking, the left in drawers and a short stocking; fool's cap; codpiece.

60. French wrestler and referee, at the time of Francis I (reigned 1515–1547), from a tapestry. Wrestler: tights and form-fitting jacket. Referee: slashed breeches, stockings, tight jacket, plumed cap.

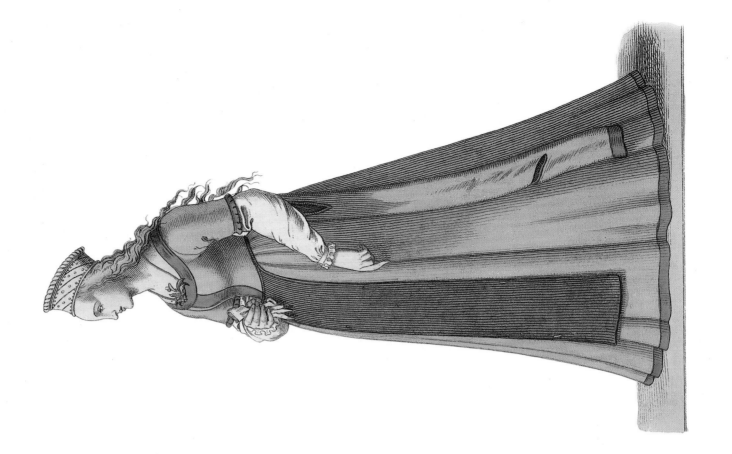

62. Young German woman from Danzig, 16th century. Silk dress; apron; gold crown, perhaps indicating she is a bride on the way to her wedding.

61. French trumpeters at a joust, reign of Francis I, from a tapestry. Long buttoned tunics with trailing sleeves that are also adjustable to the arms; jerkins beneath the tunics.

63. Flemish military attendant, from a 16th-century tapestry. Loose jacket with wide sleeves attached; hose with slashing; cap over a wide-mesh hair net.

65. Frenchwoman from Bayonne, from a 16th-century drawing. Turban with a horn and linen neckcloth; gathered dress revealing the underskirt.

64. Spanish woman from Castile, from a 1572 watercolor. Dress, with slashed sleeves, gathered to the waist and revealing the underskirt; muslin chemise and inner sleeves; clogs.

66. Young Flemish lady-in-waiting, from a 16th-century tapestry. Long, artistically draped dress with wide sleeves revealing inner sleeves; headdress with gauze, pearls and hanging ribbons.

67. Walloon soldier in Spanish service, from a 16th-century drawing. Morion-type helmet, ruff, sleeveless doublet, tight sleeves attached to an undershirt, baggy trunk hose, stockings.

68. German mercenary, from a 16th-century drawing. Long, baggy trunk hose
falling from tight drawers; doublet over shirt; tall, wide-brimmed hat.

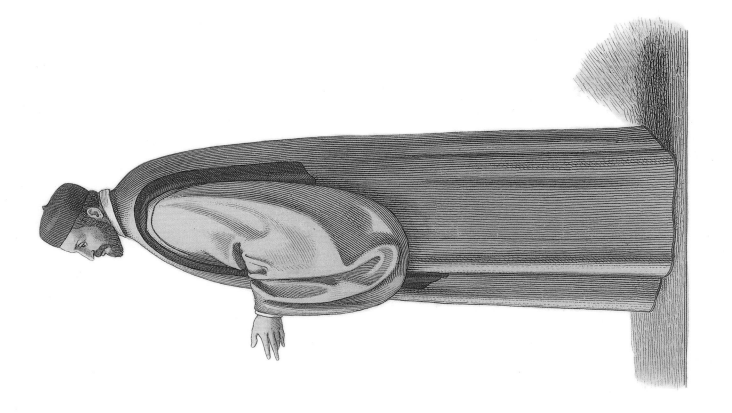

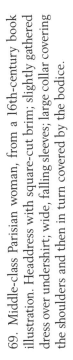

70. Venetian nobleman, from a 16th-century miniature. Long, wide-sleeved robe with stole over the shoulder; simple round hat.

69. Middle-class Parisian woman, from a 16th-century book illustration. Headdress with square-cut brim; slightly gathered dress over undershirt; wide, falling sleeves; large collar covering the shoulders and then in turn covered by the bodice.

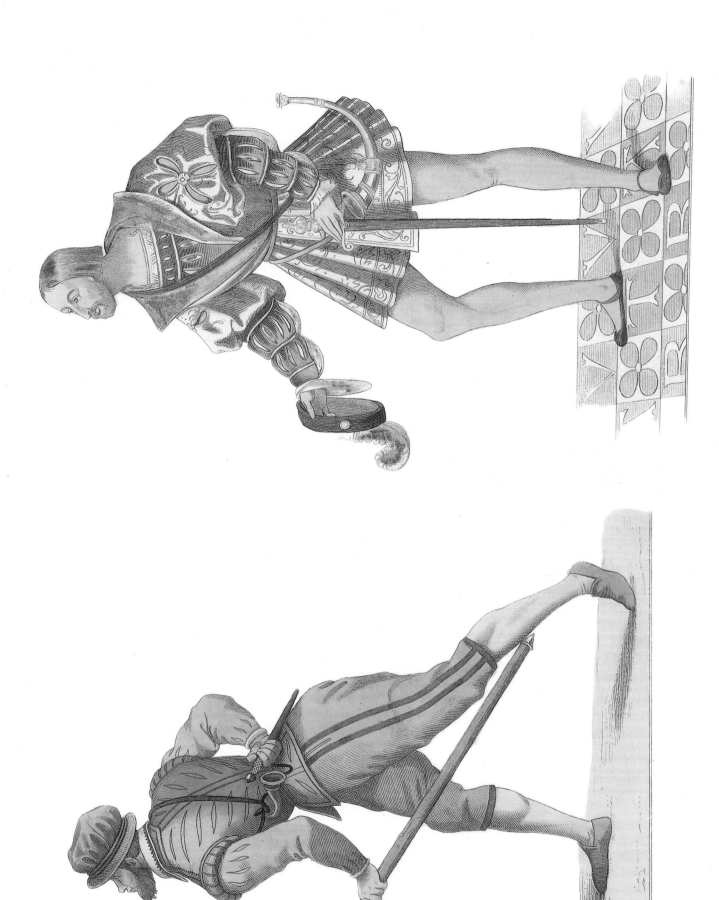

72. French nobleman of the court of Francis I (reigned 1515–1547), from a tapestry. Short silk tunic over a slashed doublet, hose.

71. French huntsman, at the time of Charles IX (reigned 1560–1574), from a print by Etienne Delaune. Slashed leather doublet over undershirt, breeches, stockings.

73. King James IV of Scotland (reigned 1488–1513), from a colored drawing. Velvet tunic, simple armor.

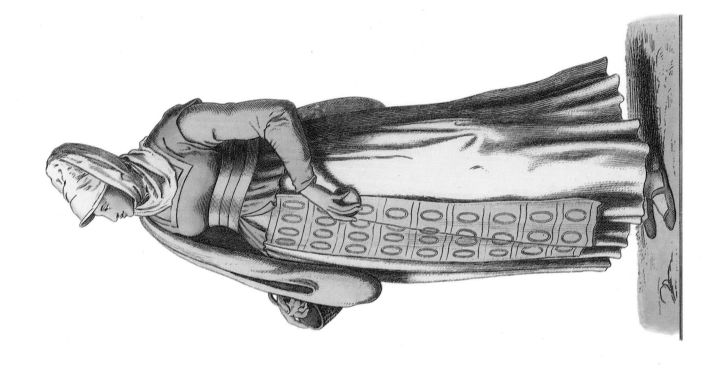

75. Portuguese countrywoman selling oranges, 16th century, from a hand-colored print. Moorish influence: sleeveless red bodice, yellow skirt, green apron, white headcloth covering the neck as well, wide belt supporting the breasts.

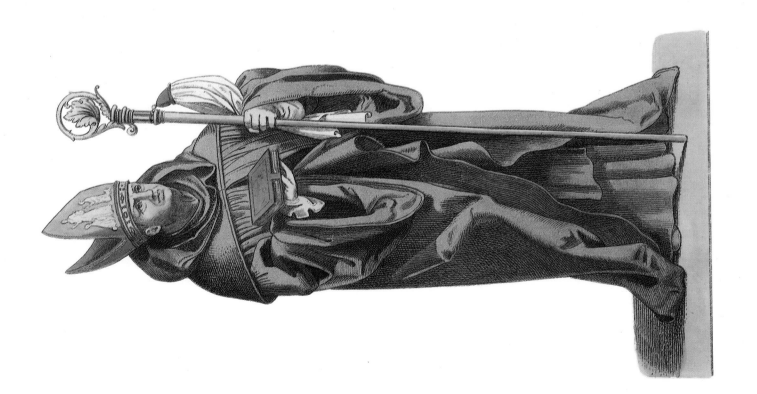

74. German Benedictine abbot, from a hand-colored woodcut of 1518. Wide robe as outerwear.

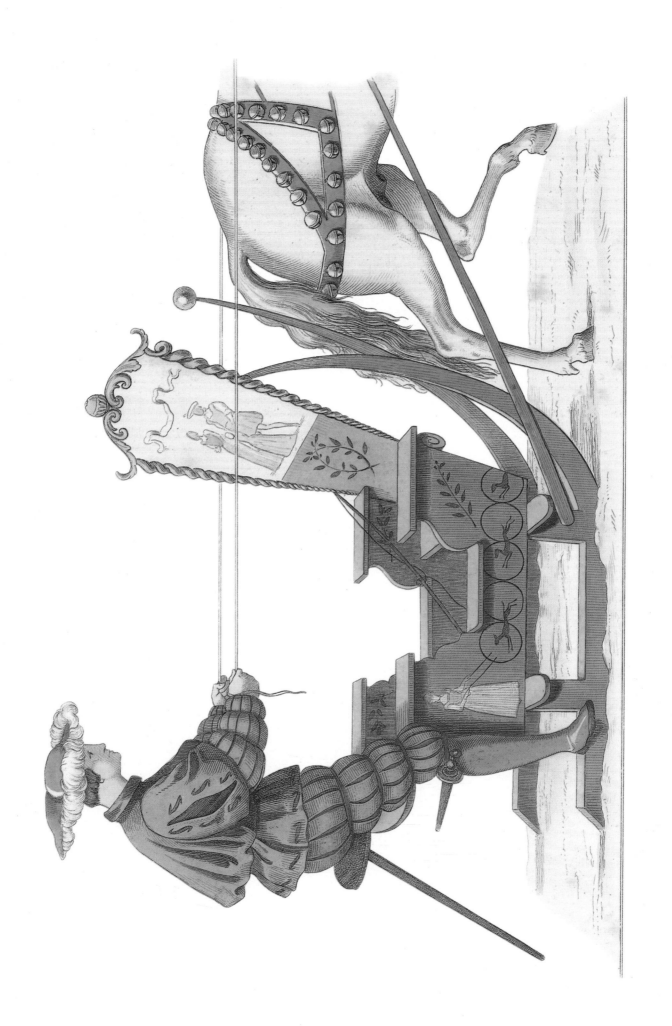

76. Matthew Schwartz, a citizen of Augsburg, Germany, participating in a sleigh race, from a 16th-century miniature.

77.  King Louis XII of France (reigned 1498–1515), from a miniature. Short robe
(*gipon*) over armor, plumed iron helmet. The horse is richly caparisoned.

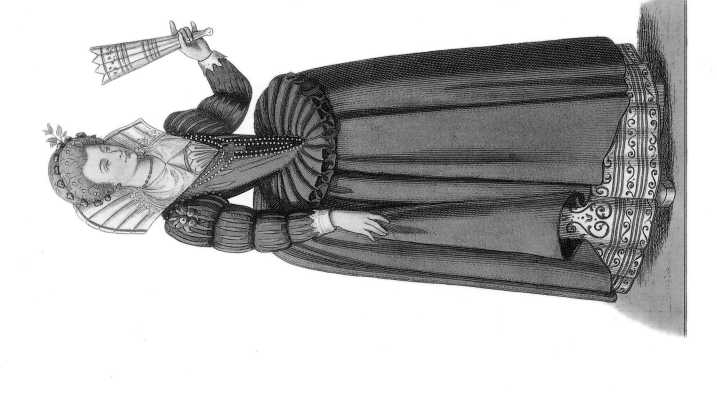

79. Young Frenchwoman, at the time of Henry III (reigned 1574–1589). Long, low-necked, pointed bodice; hip pads creating a hoopskirt effect; starched standing collar; circlet of pearls and flowers in the hair.

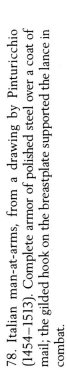

78. Italian man-at-arms, from a drawing by Pinturicchio (1454–1513). Complete armor of polished steel over a coat of mail; the gilded hook on the breastplate supported the lance in combat.

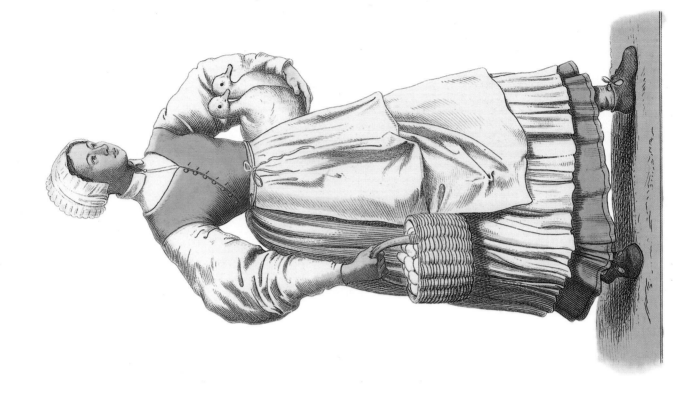

81. French peasant woman on the way to market. Side-buttoned sleeveless bodice, long skirt and underskirt, narrow apron, turndown collar, pleated bonnet.

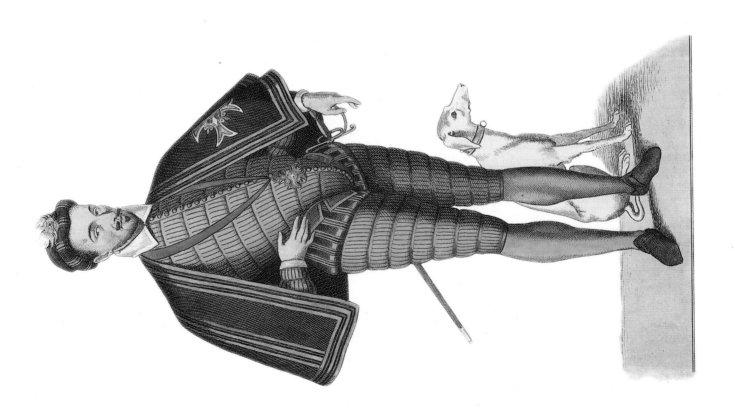

80. King Henry III of France, from a painting. Short cape, doublet, breeches, stockings, small cap.

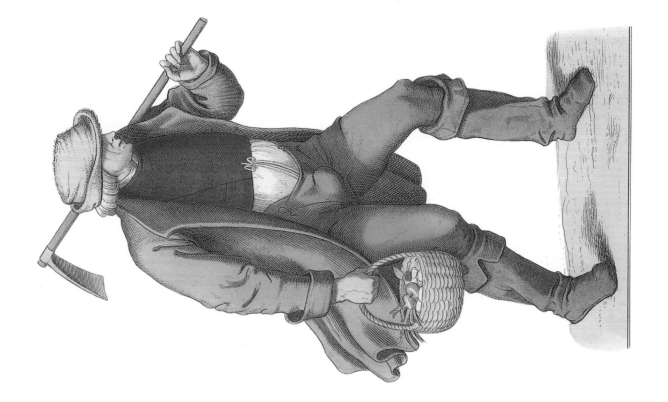

83. French peasant, from a book illustration of 1567. Heavy jacket, woolen vest, tight breeches, high leather boots, fur cap.

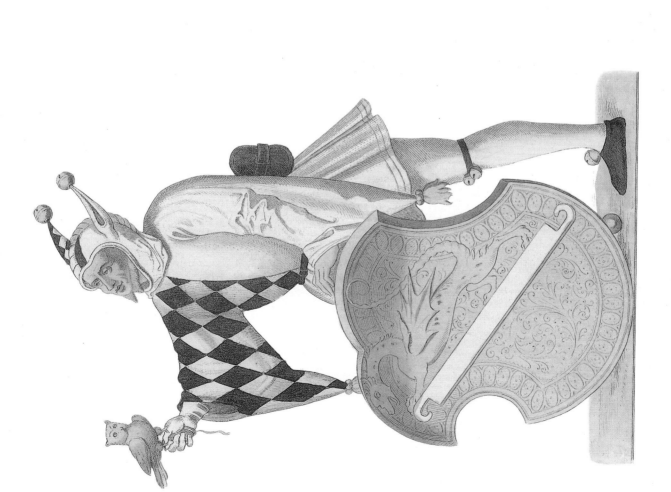

82. Swiss jester (festival costume), from a stained-glass window dated 1553. Short tunic with wide sleeves, fool's cap, tight breeches.

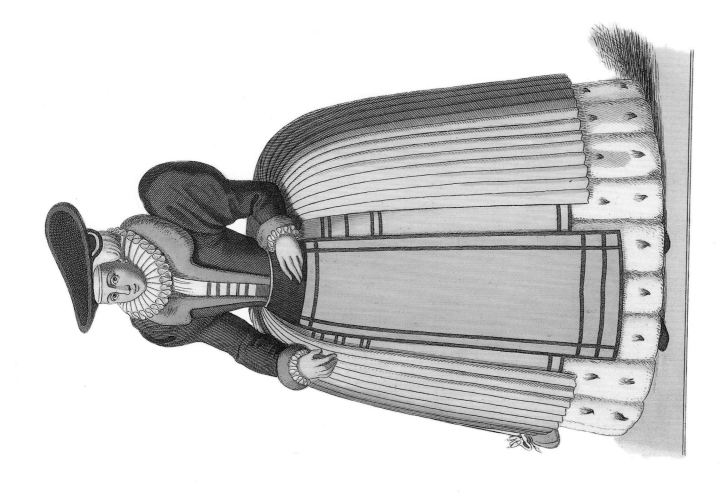

85. Alsatian woman, early 17th century, from a colored print. Two skirts, supported by farthingales, the upper one finely pleated, the lower one ermine-trimmed; apron; fur-trimmed bodice; sleeves puffed at the shoulders; ruff; typical headdress.

84. French lackey running ahead of a carriage, from a hand-colored woodcut of 1567. Slashed doublet, white jacket, trunk hose, bare knees, mid-calf-length stockings, plumed cap.

86. Swiss halberdier, from a stained-glass window of 1613. Slashed black silk doublet over a blue jacket, trunk hose, hose, broad-brimmed felt hat with plumes.

87. Spanish bishop, from a painting by Murillo (1618–1682). Wide, stiff cope over a long alb; miter.

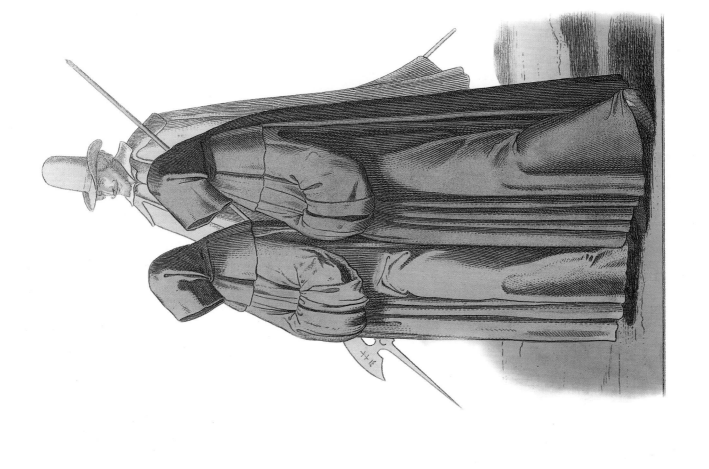

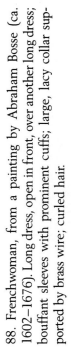

89. Male mourning costume, Lorraine, 1608, from a book illustration. Long robes and hoods.

88. Frenchwoman, from a painting by Abraham Bosse (ca. 1602–1676). Long dress, open in front, over another long dress; bouffant sleeves with prominent cuffs; large, lacy collar supported by brass wire; curled hair.

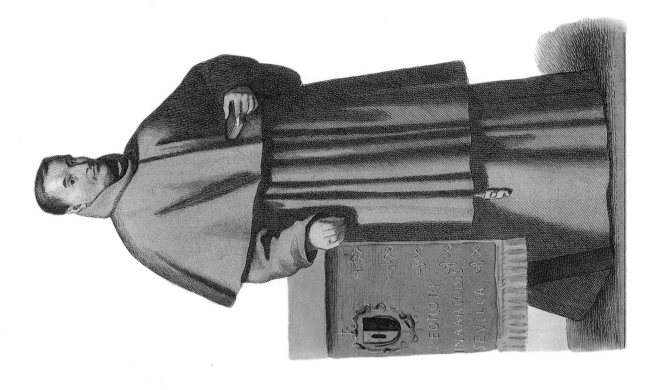

91. Pedro de Urbina, Archbishop of Seville, as a Franciscan monk, from a painting by Murillo (1618–1682). Cassock and mozzetta.

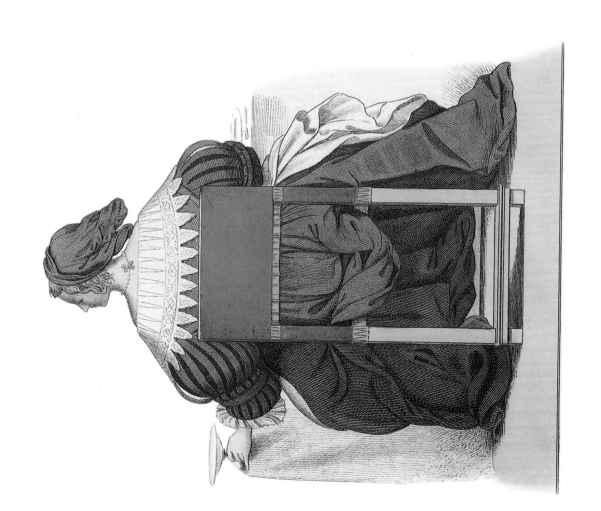

90. Frenchwoman, from a painting by Bosse (ca. 1602–1676). Very similar to no. 88, but the collar is turned down and the hairdo and head covering are entirely different.

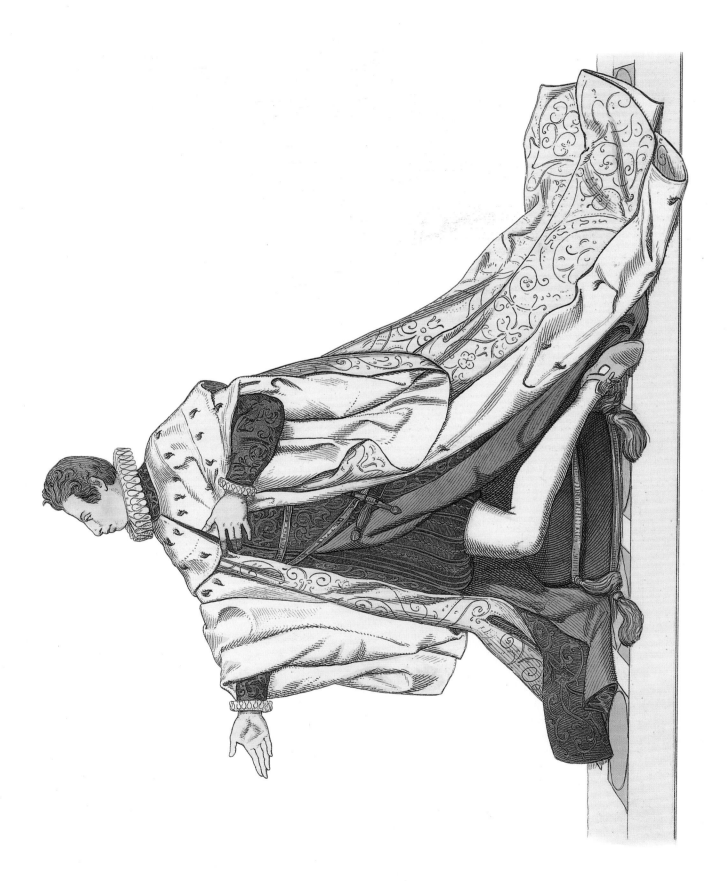

92. Cosmo II de'Medici, Grand Duke of Tuscany (reigned 1609–1621), from an encaustic painting. Long brocade suit, cloth-of-gold mantle lined with ermine, hose, ruff.

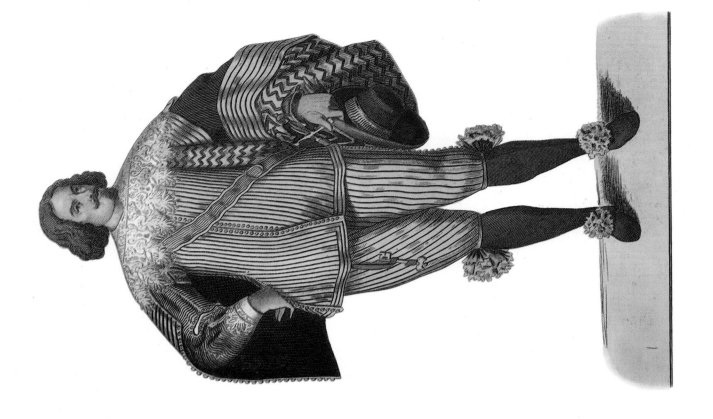

94. Italian chamberlain, 17th century. Brocade doublet and breeches, short cape, wide lace collar.

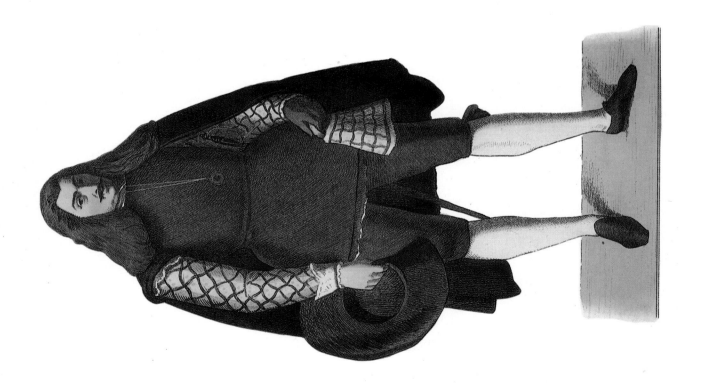

93. Spanish nobleman, from a painting by Murillo (1618–1682). Everyday visiting costume: black doublet, breeches, cape and hat; gray-and-white silk sleeves.

96. French ballet costume, from an engraving of 1660. Bodice with matching very short overskirt, ornate underskirt.

95. French nobleman in a festival costume recalling ancient Roman dress, from a 16th-century tapestry.

98. King Louis XIV of France as the Sun King in a ballet, from an engraving of 1660. Plumed cap, mantle, tunic, notched sleeves, white silk tights, low boots.

97. French ballet costume, from an engraving of 1660. Tunic, narrow at the waist; short, tight breeches; stockings; plumed beret.

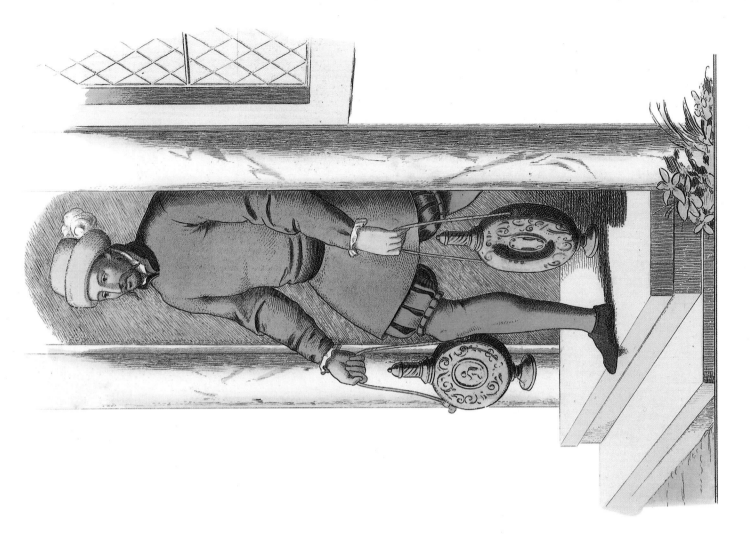

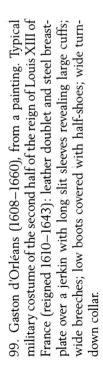

100. English valet, at the time of Edward VI (reigned 1547–1553), from a painting. Fur cap; knee-length jerkin; long, narrow sleeves; trunk hose; stockings; leather shoes.

99. Gaston d'Orléans (1608–1660), from a painting. Typical military costume of the second half of the reign of Louis XIII of France (reigned 1610–1643): leather doublet and steel breast-plate over a jerkin with long slit sleeves revealing large cuffs; wide breeches; low boots covered with half-shoes; wide turn-down collar.

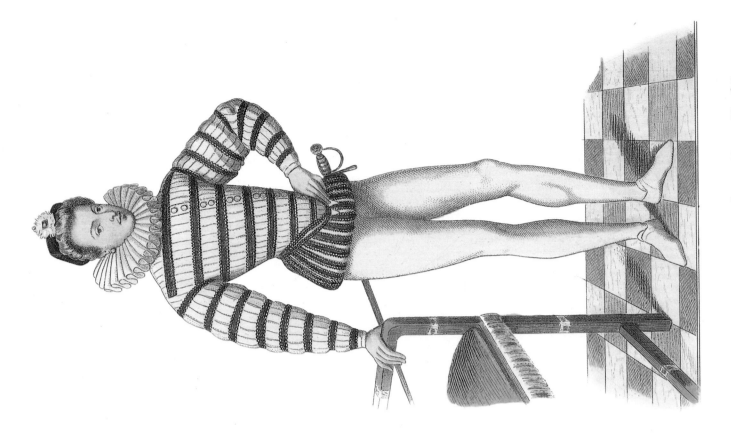

102. A mignon of the court of King Henry III of France (reigned 1574–1589), from a miniature. Doublet, very short silk trunk hose, white silk hose, ruff, black cap with jewel and plumes.

101. English nobleman and noblewoman, from a 16th-century painting. The man wears a doublet, hose and cap. The woman wears a long silk dress with bouffant sleeves, a high-collared chemise and a simple satin cap.

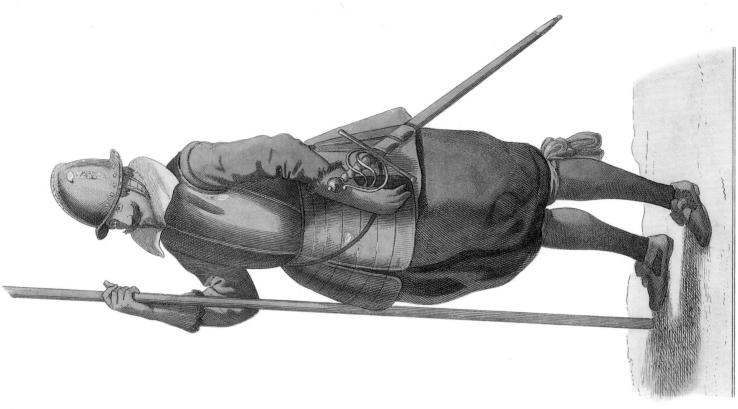

104. Pikeman, French Flanders, Louis XIII period (1610–1643), from a painting. Upper body armor with metal tassets partially covering a leather jacket, very wide breeches, stockings, morion.

103. English noblewoman, from a 16th-century painting. Velvet dress with very wide sleeves revealing muslin inner sleeves, high-collared chemise, diadem headdress.

105. English nobleman and noblewoman, from a 16th-century painting. The man wears a hooded cloak, doublet, trunk hose, hose, plumed cap. The woman wears a silk dress with short sleeves, over a chemise with a high, stiff collar; plumed hat.

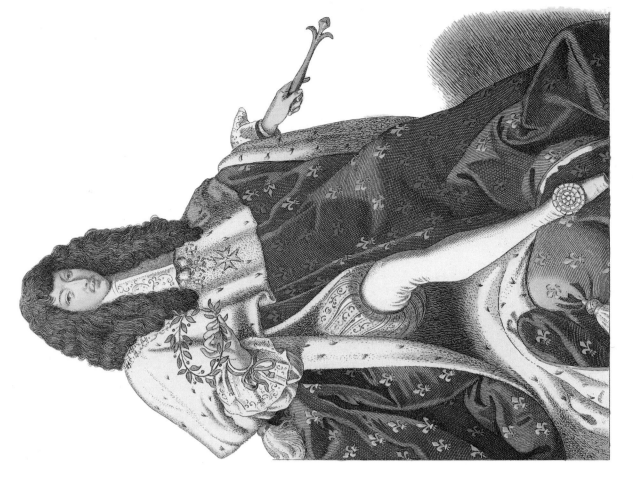

107. King Louis XIV of France at about age 22 (ca. 1660).
Ermine-lined velvet mantle.

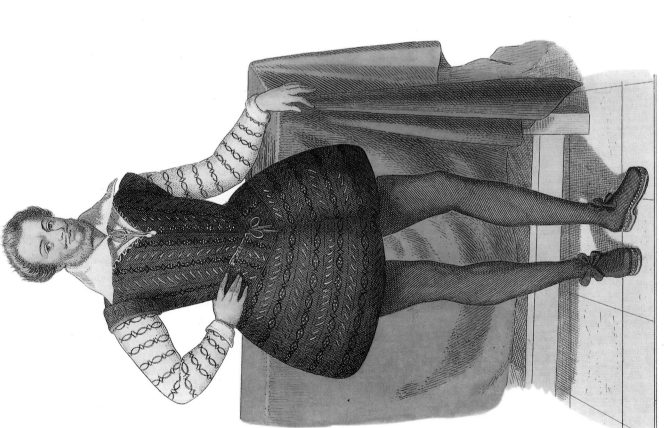

106. Antoine de Saint-Chamans, at the time of French King
Henry IV (reigned 1589–1610), from a contemporary portrait.
Doublet, silk trunk hose, turndown collar.

109. Spanish artists, from a 17th-century painting. Doublet with short tails, breeches, high boots, hanging sleeves over form-fitting sleeves, sashlike belt, wide collar.

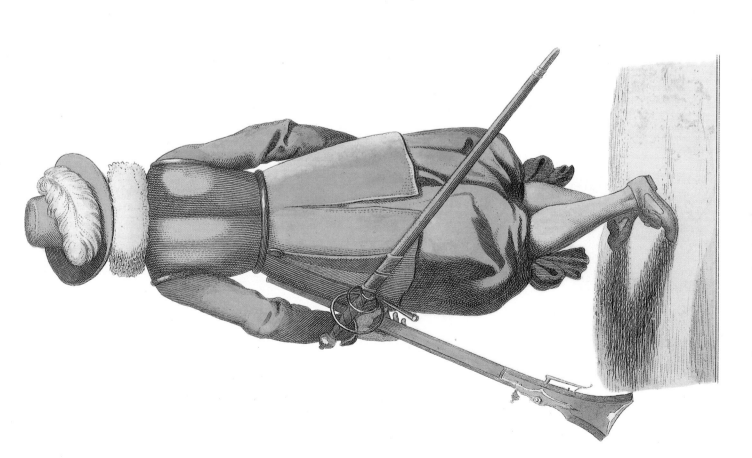

108. Musketeer, French Flanders, Louis XIII period (1610–1643), from a painting. Upper body armor, leather jacket, wide breeches, goffered collar, felt hat with plume.

111. Netherlandish officer, from a painting by David Teniers the Younger (1610–1690). Doublet, breeches, low boots with wide tops, broad-brimmed felt hat with plume, voluminous cape.

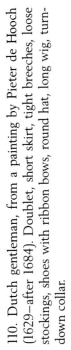

110. Dutch gentleman, from a painting by Pieter de Hooch (1629–after 1684). Doublet, short skirt, tight breeches, loose stockings, shoes with ribbon bows, round hat, long wig, turn-down collar.

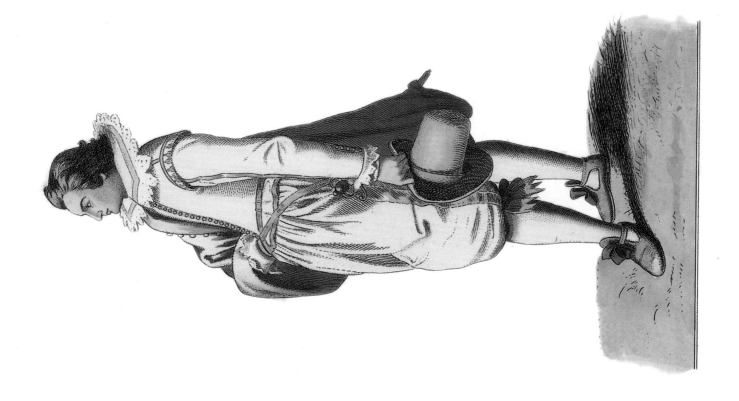

113. Young Netherlandish nobleman, from a painting by Adrian van de Venne, 1616. Doublet; long, wide breeches; cape; high felt hat; stiff collar supported by cardboard.

112. King Charles I of England, from a painting by Van Dyck, ca. 1635. White satin jacket, red velvet breeches, boots with golden spurs, turndown collar, broad-brimmed hat with plume.

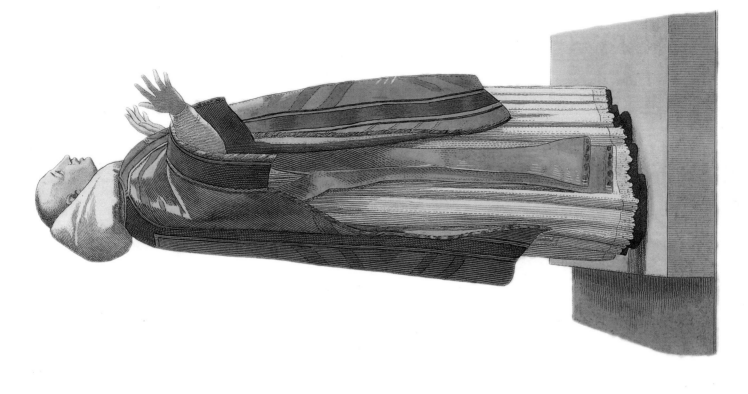

115. French deacon, from a painting by Eustache Lesueur, 1651. Cloth-of-gold dalmatic over a white alb, with a Benedictine robe beneath; stole; muslin-covered hood (amice).

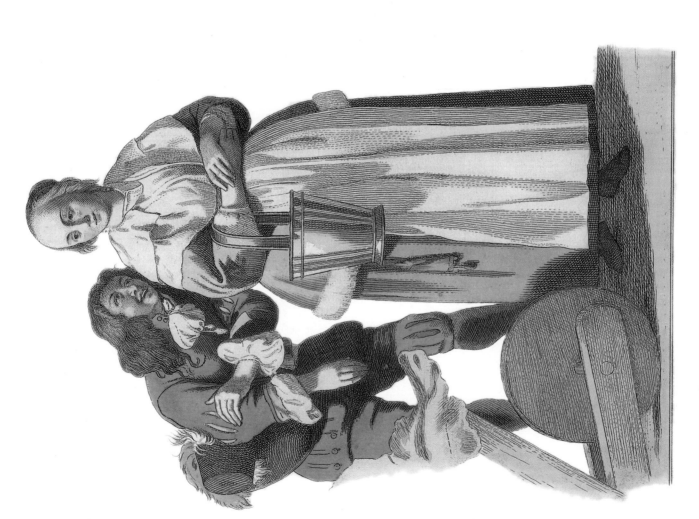

114. Well-to-do Dutch housewife and page, from a painting by Gabriel Metsu (1629–1667). She wears a swansdown-trimmed jacket with a double pelerine, and a wide apron over her skirt. He wears a red silk outfit with slashes and carries a wide hat with plume.

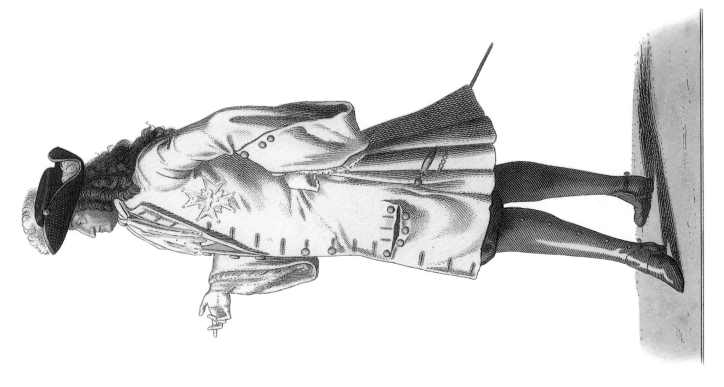

117. King Louis XIV of France, from a painting by Jean-Baptiste Martin the Elder, 1701. White jacket buttoned at the waist; wide-cuffed sleeves with lace cuffs inside; polished leather leggings attached to the shoes; long wig; beaver hat with plume; lace neckerchief.

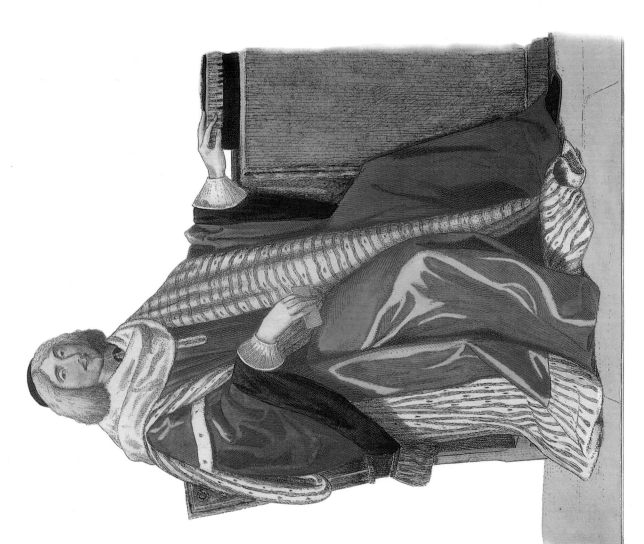

116. French judge (Jean-Antoine de Mesmes), from a painting by Philippe de Champaigne, 1653. Red robe, cape of squirrel fur, white fur hood encircling the neck, cap (mortier) held in the hand.

119. Valet attached to the French court, from a painting by J.-B. Martin, 1701. Redingote over a jacket, breeches, beaver hat, muslin cravat.

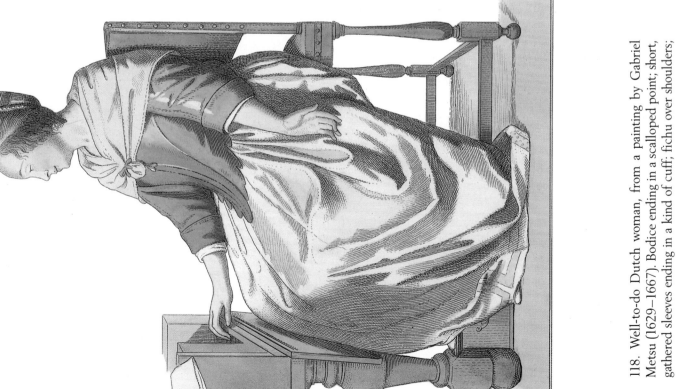

118. Well-to-do Dutch woman, from a painting by Gabriel Metsu (1629–1667). Bodice ending in a scalloped point; short, gathered sleeves ending in a kind of cuff; fichu over shoulders; hair in chignon with pearl-adorned net.

120. French cavalryman of the Louis XIII period (1610–1643), from a painting by Sébastien Bourdon. Leather jacket under a metal cuirass; very high leather boots; cape; broad-brimmed felt hat.

121. French standard-bearer of a private amateur company of harquebusiers, Louis XIII period (1610–1643), from a stained-glass window. Plumed hat, ruff, doublet, baggy breeches, beaver gloves.

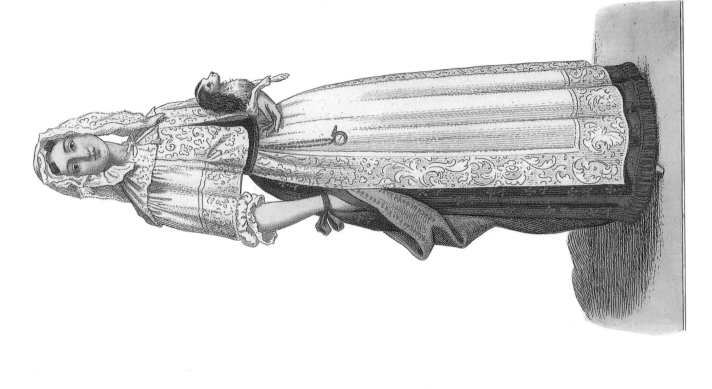

123. French upper-class woman in morning negligee, from a 17th-century print after a drawing by Jean de Saint-Jean. Lace cap, lace shoulder cape (palatine), lace-trimmed apron and another gathered overskirt in the rear.

122. Dutch youth, from a painting by Pieter van Slingeland (1640–1691). Short doublet revealing the shirt at the waistline, skirtlike breeches known as a rhinegrave, knee ornaments known as canions, large turndown collar, beaver hat.

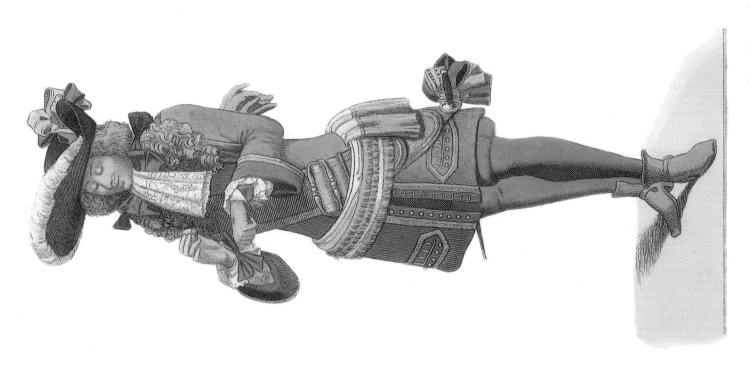

125. French officer of the king, from a 1675 print after a drawing by Jean de Saint-Jean. Cloth-of-gold baldric over the jacket, sash at hip level, ribboned collar and cuffs, large blond wig, wide beaver hat.

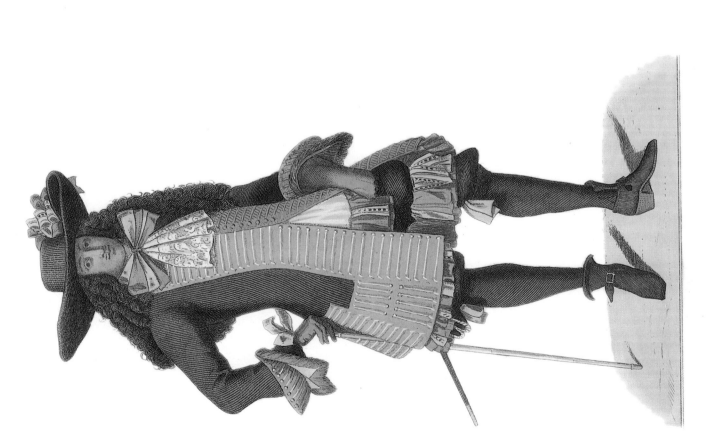

124. French nobleman, from a 17th-century print after a drawing by Jean de Saint-Jean. Jacket with heavy gold and silver embroidery and double cuffs, cravat over a turndown collar, knee breeches, canions, stockings, shoes with high red heels, long wig, broad-brimmed beaver hat, long gloves.

127. French peasant in going-to-town clothes, from a 1679 print after a drawing by Jean de Saint-Jean. Gray redingote over a yellow-brown outfit; stockings; leather shoes; felt hat.

126. French upper-class woman in visiting dress, from a 17th-century print after a drawing by Jean de Saint-Jean. Dress with train, with long black satin overskirt in the rear; bodice with very short sleeves revealing elbow-length lace sleeves; a broad lace band, like a bertha, around shoulders; elaborate hairdo.

128. Frenchwoman in summer attire, from a 1676 print after a drawing by Jean de Saint-Jean. Two-part headdress; silk dress composed of a long skirt and a combination bodice/short, gathered overskirt; elbow-length gloves; hanging from the belt, a satin mask as protection against wind and oglers; reed walking stick.

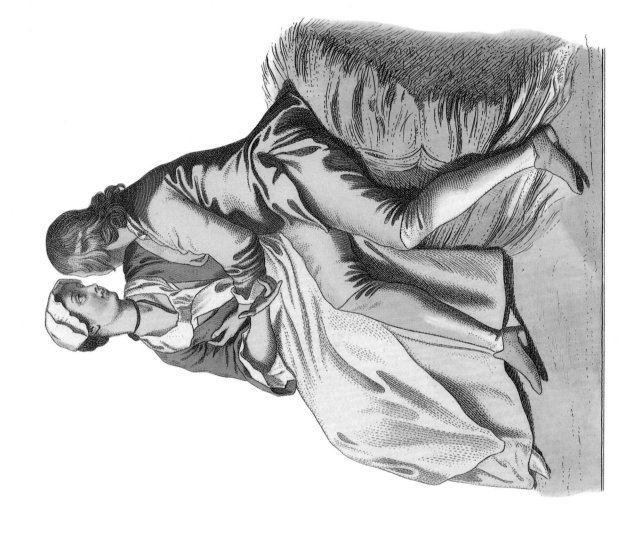

130. Young village couple, from a painting by Nicolas Lancret (1690–1743). She wears an apron over her skirt and a blue shift under her red dress. He wears a short jacket with matching knee breeches, and leather shoes.

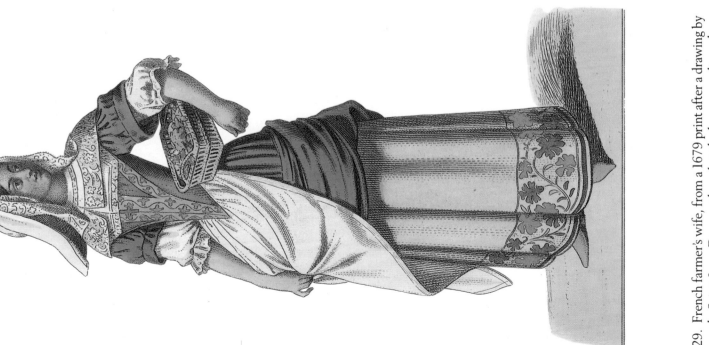

129. French farmer's wife, from a 1679 print after a drawing by Jean de Saint-Jean. Dress gathered at the knee, revealing a long underskirt; apron; lace-trimmed headdress and pelerine.

131. French huntsman/groom, from a 1737 painting by Carle van Loo. Velvet coat and breeches, striped gaiters. The pack mule is extravagantly adorned.

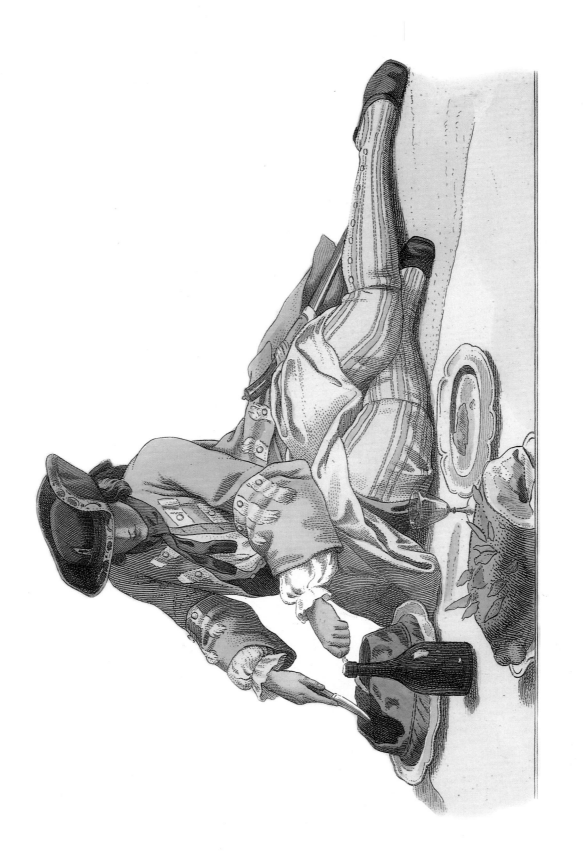

132. French nobleman in hunting attire, from a 1737 painting by Carle van Loo. Coat, breeches, gaiters, hat similar to a tricorne.

133. Venetians dressed for the local celebration of the Feast of the Ascension, from a 1750 painting. Voluminous robe and the hooded pelerine known as a *bautta*.

134. Venetian woman and dancing master, from a painting by Pietro Longhi (1702–1785). She wears a double bodice and elaborate cuffs. He wears a powdered wig and a coat with gilded buttons.

135. Italian peasant from Lombardy, from a painting by Francesco Londonio (1723–1783). Sleeveless jacket, breeches cut at knee level, shapeless felt hat.

137. Italian countrywoman from the outskirts of Milan, from a painting by Francesco Londonio (1723–1783). Low-cut bodice, skirt, sheepskin apron, kerchief completely covering the hair.

136. Governor of the port of Marseilles and a lady, from a 1754 painting by Joseph Vernet. She wears a dress with open bodice revealing a low-cut, lacy inner bodice; lacy cuffs; two skirts of the same color; small ruff. He wears a white coat over his jacket and knee breeches; a tricorne; lace jabot and cuffs.

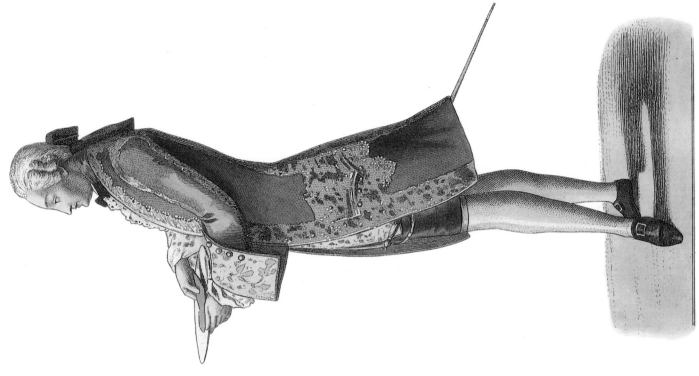

139. The French Count de Jarnac, from a painting of the 1760s or 1770s by a painter named Olivier. Velvet coat, flowered waistcoat, knee breeches, stockings, shoes, powdered hair.

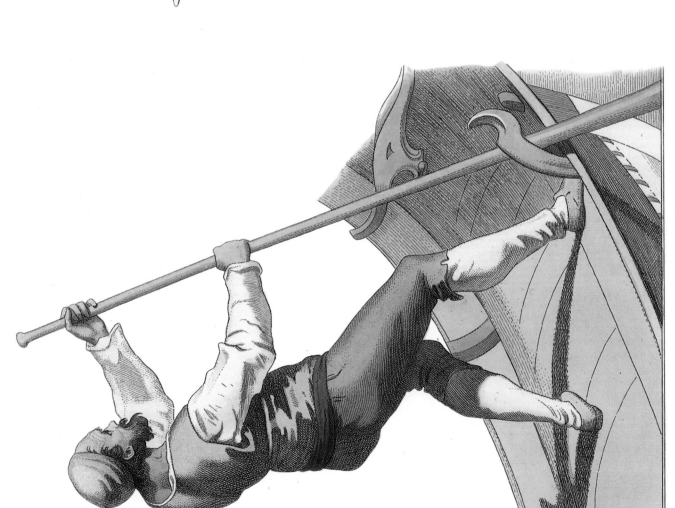

138. Venetian gondolier, from a 1750 painting by Canaletto and Domenico Tiepolo. Sleeveless jacket, knee breeches, skullcap.

140. Member of the Gardes-Françaises regiment, from a 1778 drawing by an artist named Hoffmann. Blue coat; red jacket, collar and cuffs (with white Brandenburgs); white breeches and gaiters; fur shako with white plume.

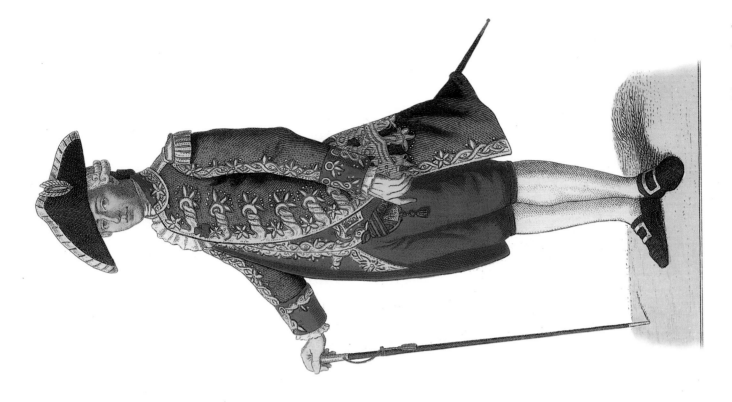

142. The French Count de Vergennes, captain of the guards of the king's residence, from a 1786 print by Hoffmann. Embroidered coat, knee breeches, tricorne.

141. French woman in ballgown, ca. 1778–1780. Skirt supported by enormous panniers and heavily trimmed with yellow silk, ending in a lacy flounce; low-necked, pointed bodice; powdered hair.

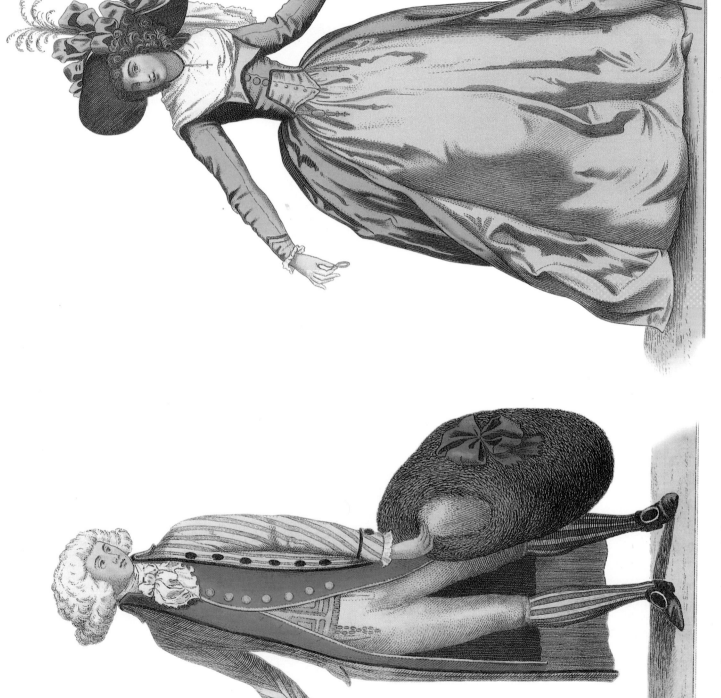

143. French dandy of the Louis XVI period, from a 1787 fashion publication. Redingote over coat over waistcoat and knee breeches; socks; cravat and jabot; in his right hand, a hat with cockade; in his left, a huge muff.

144. French middle-class woman, 1780s, from a print. Blue silk skirt covered by a pink silk "redingote" dress revealing a yellow vest; white muslin fichu; wide hat with a mass of ribbons; ebony walking stick.

146. Ferdinand Guillemardet, French ambassador to Spain, Directoire period, from a painting by Goya, ca. 1798. Blue coat and breeches, red sash with tricolor fringe, round hat with tricolor plume.

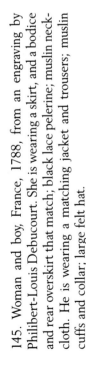

145. Woman and boy, France, 1788, from an engraving by Philibert-Louis Debucourt. She is wearing a skirt, and a bodice and rear overskirt that match; muslin pelerine; black lace neckcloth. He is wearing a matching jacket and trousers; muslin cuffs and collar; large felt hat.

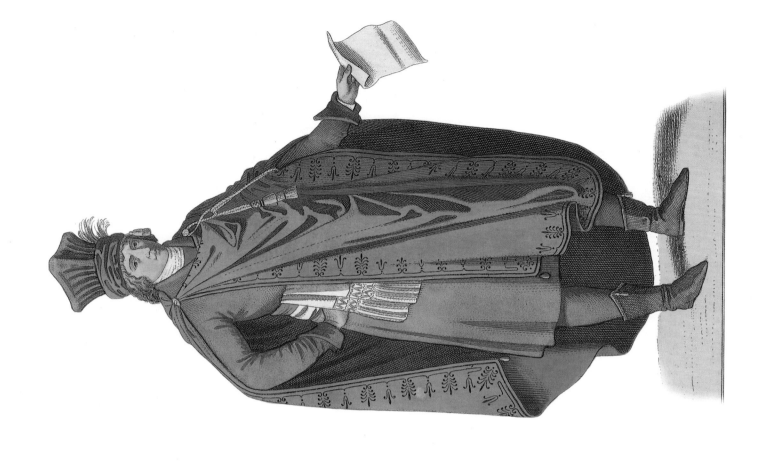

148. France; representative in the Council of 500, from a colored print ca. 1797. Cape over a long coat; tricolor silk sash; high velvet hat with tricolor aigrette.

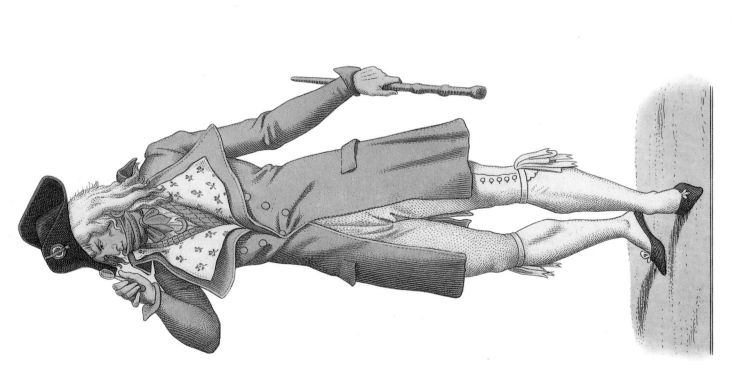

147. French dandy ("incroyable") of the Directoire period (1795–1799), from a work by Carle Vernet. Redingote with two rows of buttons; standing collar; large lapels; pointed cuffs; waistcoat with lapels; breeches buttoned at the knee; earrings; gold crescent shirt pin; knotted stick; cravat; felt hat; long wig.

149. French ultrafashionable woman ("merveilleuse") of the Directoire period (1795–1799), from a work by Carle Vernet. Long dress, gathered up to the calf; jonquil-yellow shawl; elbow-length gloves worn loosely on the forearm; jockey hat with extremely long visor; unbound, powdered hair; cravat covering the chin.

150. England; the Prince of Wales, later King George IV, as Knight of the Garter, from a color drawing by Adam Buck, 1799. Garter; gold chain; cloak with motto; cordon; plumed hat.